Writing for Study Purposes

A teacher's guide to developing individual writing skills

Arthur Brookes
Peter Grundy

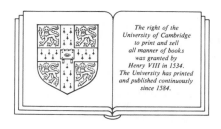

The right of the
University of Cambridge
to print and sell
all manner of books
was granted by
Henry VIII in 1534.
The University has printed
and published continuously
since 1584.

Cambridge University Press
Cambridge
New York   Port Chester
Melbourne   Sydney

An earlier version of this book, entitled *Designer Writing*, was published by Pilgrims Publications, Canterbury, England. In this Cambridge University Press volume the original text has been substantially revised and expanded.

This title was prepared with Roger Bowers as consultant editor.

Published by the Press Syndicate of the University of Cambridge
The Pitt Building, Trumpington Street, Cambridge CB2 1RP
40 West 20th Street, New York, NY 10011, USA
10 Stamford Road, Oakleigh, Melbourne 3166, Australia

© Cambridge University Press 1990

First published 1990

Printed in Great Britain
by Bell & Bain, Glasgow

British Library cataloguing in publication data

Brookes, Arthur
Writing for study purposes ; a teacher's guide to
developing individual writing skills.
1. English. Language. Writing skills. Teaching
I. Title   II. Grundy, Peter
808.04207

ISBN 0 521 35325 4 hardcover
ISBN 0 521 35853 1 paperback

CE

Contents

PART 1   THE APPROACH

Contents

PART 2   THE EXERCISES

The authors

At present we work in the University of Durham but have at one time or another taught in a number of other institutions both in Britain and overseas. In Durham itself an important part of our teaching has been to provide language input classes for overseas students. As these students (many of whom are working towards a Ph.D. by research) advance in work in their chosen fields, they become increasingly concerned about their difficulties in fully conveying their intended meaning in written English.

We were faced with a choice of conventional teaching of English for Academic Purposes at this level, or of setting writing firmly within a communicative approach using humanistic methodology. We found that it was, in fact, very helpful for all our serious learners when we employed largely humanistic, learner-centred methodology and avoided a concentration on matching up to a notional ideal product. It is these ideas which we hope to share in this book. Because we have found them helpful, we hope others may find them equally useful in both general language teaching and specialist EAP work. Although our own experience has been with overseas students working in a British university – and many of the examples in our text are drawn from this context – we believe that our ideas and the approach we offer will have wider currency. The final section offers some suggestions.

Arthur Brookes
Peter Grundy

Acknowledgements

We wish to thank very many people for their help with this book. Mostly our students in Durham, both language learners and applied linguists, who have helped with development of both philosophy and materials and who have taught us to believe in a truly process based approach to the teaching of writing. We also owe a debt to colleagues in the School of English in Durham and to the English Language Professor, Charles Jones, who have given us the opportunity to work co-operatively and has granted us leave from teaching to develop our ideas and write about them.

We also owe much to John Morgan and Mario Rinvolucri whose encouragement, comments and example we greatly value. We are grateful too to Roger Bowers, whose initial encouragement, careful reading of our drafts and thoughtful comments were invaluable. Annemarie Young and Lindsay White at CUP provided literally hundreds of extremely detailed and insightful comments over many months, which certainly did much to improve our first (and several subsequent) manuscripts. The financial support of the University of Durham Staff Travel Fund and the British Council enabled us to pilot materials in an extremely productive and intensive week at the University of Warsaw, where staff and students of the English Faculty gave much advice. Where particular exercises incur debts, they are acknowledged in the body of the book. All the remaining faults are our own.

Every effort has been made to obtain permission to use the cartoon on page 104 which was published in *Over the Line* by Russell Brockbank, Temple Press, 1958. The publishers have been unable to trace the copyright holder and would welcome information.

Preface

Some books on teaching grow out of the personal experience of their authors. Others tend to be a selection of the ideas that are currently being talked about and published. This book is of the first kind. The ideas in it have been tried out in different situations in Britain and Europe with a good deal of success. However, most ideas books for teachers need to be modified in different circumstances, and this is always easier to do when the original context of the work is known. This is why we are starting with a description of the work we do in our own institution.

We are colleagues working in a small British university. Part of our time is spent in teaching writing courses to students on in-sessional courses who are studying subjects other than English, mostly at the post-graduate level. The kind of writing that our students are typically asked to produce includes laboratory reports, essays, dissertations and doctoral theses.

Both of us have taught English at a variety of levels to native speaker, ESL and EFL learners. Generally we have favoured humanistic methodology in our teaching. What we have come to realize is that this kind of methodology is less often applied to writing, especially in support writing classes of the kind we teach. Having taken the risk ourselves and tried it out, we soon became convinced that it could play a major role in such classes.

There were two things about our particular circumstances that made it especially applicable. The first is that our classes typically consisted of students doing different subjects. It was difficult to find an academic topic to write about that would equally suit students doing business studies, theology, and applied physics. The second is that our students come from very different parts of the world with different linguistic backgrounds and different capabilities. Ours are real mixed background, mixed interest, and mixed ability classes! So we were driven to use these differences as a resource and to capitalize on students' interest in themselves and each other.

Another equally important constraint is that, in term time, students have just two hours per week for a writing class on top of all their other academic commitments. And even then attendance tends to be erratic as other unforeseen academic commitments arise. This means that each session has to be more or less self-contained and cannot involve students in writing long, complete, separate assignments for the English class. So we had to find smaller, meaningful tasks that were very often part of a lesson that had an oral as well as a written element. Our enrolment for each class is rarely more than 25, but there are always too many students for us to contemplate working with individuals on their theses or assignments.

This gave us the idea of focusing on aspects of the process of writing, and devising with the co-operation of the students a syllabus for a nine or ten session unit. Such a syllabus typically focuses on what the particular group of students decides is most important at the time, and may well consist of nine or ten relatively separate ideas. One of those ideas, included (after negotiation), in our last course, was 'comparison'. In the session on ways of comparing, we first asked each student to fill in a questionnaire about their last eating experience (see exercise 27, *Comparison – similarity and difference*). Then the students paired up and each pair wrote a paragraph comparing and contrasting their eating experiences. This is the paragraph one pair actually wrote:

When you eat in company you are likely to enjoy the better meal eaten more slowly. We illustrate this with Agnieska and Raimundo's most recent eating experience which is quite similar but also different. Both meals were well balanced, in two parts and eaten at the same time. But that is all the similarity between us. Agnieska's meal was in the restaurant with friends eaten slowly and with hot and cold courses. But Raimundo's was a snack alone eaten quickly in the laboratory.

Each paragraph was then read aloud. In the discussion which followed, the students were interested to discover:
– how comparison and contrast go hand in hand;
– how many different examples of the language of comparison had been used and how varied they were;
– how even the simplest things (such as a sandwich lunch) may be compared with a high degree of subtlety;
– how it is the writer who decides just what is worth comparing and how it should be done.

The discussion then turned to the kind of contexts outside the language classroom in which students need to make comparisons in writing. Some members of the class confessed to having been slipshod in the past, and several commented on how what they had learned in the language classroom would help them in their next piece of academic writing.

There are a number of things to notice about this particular lesson. The first is that on this occasion the raising of the students' consciousness was felt to be more important than a great deal of connected writing in the

English class. The discussion time at the end of the lesson was an essential follow-up because it enabled the students to see the relationship between what they had enjoyed doing in class and how they would need to write in their specialist subject.

Though we usually keep to this kind of methodology, we are open to using other methods from time to time. For instance, in a recent session one of us used three techniques in a two-hour session. First, having earlier been asked to deal with abstracts, he used a variation of exercise 18 (*How does an abstract differ from a summary?*). Then he used a reformulation of a page from a thesis of one of the students in the group, and finally he took a page from the work of another student, photocopied it for the class and noted the possible improvements that could be made and the reasons for them. About fifteen per cent of the class found the reformulation most helpful, about fifteen per cent the annotated page, and about seventy per cent preferred the exercise on abstracts and summaries.

In our institution over a period of several years we have come to know well the sorts of problems faced by our students as they struggle with academic writing and this has resulted in the particular set of focuses that we have provided for the exercises. However, each institution will differ and there is no reason why the list of focuses should not be extended to cover other points as well. Furthermore, there is too much material in the second half of this book to be used on any one writing course. We, therefore, select from the material after discussion with each separate group of students, and we would expect others to do the same.

It is clear that the bulk of extended writing is done in the students' main subject areas and our task is to service and improve that writing. This means that each exercise does not so much relate to the next exercise as to the body of writing being done elsewhere. So one lesson need not logically lead to the next. So how does any one exercise fit into the total work of a particular student in an institution?

Let us take someone who is finding difficulty with the many sophisticated ways of comparing two things – whether these are two economic strategies for dealing with inflation or two different types of peas that botanists are testing for growing in dry conditions. Rather than provide long lists of possible ways of showing degrees of similarity and dissimilarity, we as teachers may try something like the exercise described earlier in this preface. That might be step one, the consciousness-raising step if you like. Where appropriate, we can certainly go beyond the kind of discussion we had with our class about ways of relating our work on comparisons to the main subject. For example, pairs could be asked to underline the comparing expressions in their paragraphs and then attach these to the wall. The first range of expressions will come from the displayed phrases. One possible development is as follows. These expressions can be discussed, expecially in the light of the uses that students may find for them in their subjects. So far all the language has come from the students' combined experience and knowledge which is greater than that of any individual student while being more manageable and relevant than a complete list of all the possible expressions. There is still one more absolutely crucial stage. Students are encouraged to look at the literature in their subject to see what other expressions are used to show comparison. Another phase may well be to share these findings with others in a reporting-back session in the next lesson. Other possibilities are for students to go through their own past assignments to see how they have dealt with such comparisons in them and how they might have done it more efficiently. It is, of course, also part of the work of any language specialist working in a support context to see that reference works about language are available and their correct use made known – so that, for instance, reference can be made to a good EFL dictionary to check in which ways a particular expression is likely to be used.

If you are working on other types of courses in British institutions, whether these are pre-sessional, subject specific, or general English courses, you may well choose to modify the approach to include more detailed follow-up work, different focuses, some further continuous writing tasks where these are not catered for elsewhere as they are in our institution, or guidance in such study-skill activities as making notes of different kinds from books and articles.

If you are working outside Britain, it is worth noting that the exercises were originally designed for students in British institutions. This does not mean that they will not work elsewhere. We have already piloted many of them successfully overseas. You may, however, have to adapt exercises in some of these ways:
– Where the teaching style is normally fairly formal the exercises need to be introduced gradually starting with the ones you are happiest with.
– Some of the exercises refer to circumstances of daily life in Britain, such as British food, weather, or holidays; all of these can be easily replaced where appropriate by similar local topics.
– Where the conditions in a particular classroom make movement difficult it is possible, in some exercises, to change the suggested group size and to make the act of fixing pieces of writing to the wall and subsequent reading more formalized. For example, one of the class can put material up and read the results out to the class – not an ideal solution but still a possible one.

Conclusion

We hope it has been a help that we have shared with you the personal motivation for the approach taken in this book with some indication of its general adaptability to a wide variety of different institutions. It would complete our own continuing evaluation and development of this approach if you would share with us the successes and difficulties you find as you apply these ideas in your own circumstances.

Arthur Brookes
Peter Grundy
School of English, University of Durham

Introduction

1   Teaching writing communicatively

We believe that an approach to the teaching of writing that combines communicative practice, an integrated approach and humanistic principles is both overdue and not so difficult to accomplish as previously thought. Put diagrammatically, what is required looks something like this:

Although we have not yet carefully defined what is meant by communicative practice, an integrated approach or humanistic principles, we suspect that there is a general sympathy for these ideas. To what extent, then, have they impinged on the teaching of writing?

Many teachers feel that writing has been the poor relation in the language teaching developments of the last ten years. Any widely travelled teacher-trainer will have been struck by the number of teachers who acknowledge the very real importance of writing, but despair of finding interesting ways of teaching it. Many teachers feel they are on top of communicative approaches to listening, speaking and, to a considerable extent, reading too, but that the key to teaching writing communicatively eludes them. This book attempts to meet that need.

It also recognizes a second difficulty in teaching writing, which stems from the fact that the writing process involves making choices between several possible ways of making a point. For non-native speaker teachers in particular, this can be a real problem since an awareness of the possible options and of the criteria for choosing between them is not always present. For this reason, the writing exercises we suggest are designed to place the non-native speaker teacher on an equal footing with his or her native speaker counterpart.

Communicative practice

We exemplify some of the features of good communicative practice in relation to teaching spoken language under the six sub-headings below. We focus on teaching spoken language at this stage because it will be most familiar to our readers.

Having something meaningful to say: A classroom is not communicative just because the learners are talking to each other. They could be acting out a model dialogue, for example, or rehearsing a role play. Indeed, this sort of artificial, imitative work is all too often styled as communicative. It is central to the communicative approach that learners exchange meanings and express opinions that are their own. This is to be contrasted with the use of the term meaningful to refer to working with a vocabulary of supposed relevance, usually built around taxis, hotels, airports and shopping. In a genuinely communicative classroom, learners use meaningful talk to represent the way they think and feel and to relate their knowledge and experience of the world to others.

Reaching an audience: As well as having something worth saying, learners also need to be able to get this message across to someone else. This calls for opportunities to practise trying to make oneself fully understood by other learners.

Working in small groups: This is particularly important because it allows each learner to speak more often than when the class works as a whole. The size of a group also determines the type of communicative activity that can take place (e.g., pairs are needed for a dialogue, small groups for a discussion, etc.).

Working collaboratively: Wherever there is a two-way communication, there will be collaborative interaction. In a language learning context, this implies the opportunity for self-monitoring, self-repair, and peer correction.

Developing register awareness: When we talk, we do not only convey literal meanings. The difference between 'Got the time, mate?' and 'Excuse me, you haven't by any chance got the time, have you?' is not one of literal meaning. In each case, the speakers reveal something about themselves and the relationships they think they have with their hearers. Such differences in register enable us to capture relationships of power and distance in the language we use. To communicate appropriately, learners too must be able to encode the perceived distance and any power inequalities between themselves and their interlocutors.

Talking naturally: A natural conversation is not one whose final form is known at the outset. Learners will be organizing their thoughts as they talk. Talking is a process.

Thus the 'communicative practice' box in the previous diagram might now be more explicitly defined:

communicative practice	=	having something meaningful to say reaching an audience working in small groups working collaboratively developing register awareness talking naturally

It is noticeable that many of these central communicative practices apply not only to teaching spoken language but also to teaching writing. You cannot write without having something meaningful to convey, without knowing and reaching an audience, without being aware of appropriate register and variety, for example. Furthermore, a writing classroom set up for collaborative group work will provide a readership (fellow-students) and an opportunity for rewriting so as to enable the accurate expression of the intended meaning. And although a written text will ultimately achieve a final form, working on the process of achieving this final product involves organizing one's thoughts as one writes.

An integrated approach

Following an integrated approach does not mean working on the same text in each of the four modes in turn as in audio-lingualism. Nor does it mean merely working with a textbook that affords space to each skill. It means recognizing that in the real world we are rarely exercising only one skill at a time. If, for example, we take a telephone message, we are listening, speaking, writing the message down and reading it back in an integrated display of multi-skill competence. The purpose of an integrated approach in the classroom is to enable learners to transfer naturally between one mode and another, so that they do not end up like student A who passes the written exam but cannot ask for a sandwich, or student B who talks fluently but whose reading and writing skills are so limited that written messages have to be read aloud in order to be understood. These all too common symptoms show that teaching each skill separately very often results in unbalanced second language performance.

Thus our integrated approach box too might be more explicitly defined:

an integrated approach	=	transferring naturally between one skill and another

If we had a pound for every occasion students on our EAP writing courses complained of their very real difficulties in incorporating what they had heard or read into their writing, we would have taken early retirement long ago. This must be the strongest argument for a multi-skill approach to the teaching of writing. Sometimes we will want the skills to be sequenced, as in extracting information from a text before writing about it, and sometimes simultaneous, as in listening and note taking.

Similarly, there will be occasions when we would expect group or even whole class discussion to be an integral part of the writing class. So if an hour's discussion led to only a single sentence of writing, one would not necessarily think it was time wasted. This will be the exception, of course, but it serves to remind us that to ask individuals to attempt a writing task in isolation assumes that they know what to do, and can write effectively and accurately already. In that sense, writing demands an integrated approach just as much as the other skills do.

Humanistic principles

In this section we will not be discussing any of the particular method-ologies to which the humanistic label has been attached (the silent way, suggestopedia and so on). Rather, we will be trying to establish some of the general principles of humanistic teaching which follow from seeing the person at the centre of things, and from always thinking first of the learner and second of what is to be learnt. It will, of course, be a far from exhaustive description.

The learner's freedom to express himself or herself is clearly a central humanistic principle. This involves a number of sub-principles, among them:
— Seeing the learner as the main resource both of meanings (things to talk about) and language (ways of talking).
— Recognizing that the learner should be free from authority, prescrip-tion, overt correction and, according to some in the humanistic movement, the imposition of language models.
— Understanding the vital need to create a context in which the learner's self-expression is encouraged and respected.
A person-related approach recognizes the learner as an individual with intelligence, feelings, experiences, knowledge and information, in short, as a person with a biography — and seizes on this biography as a vital resource in the learning process. It sees learning a language as a total experience and as a personal discovery with implications for commit-ment of time and energy, as well as for self-image, sense of cultural belonging, and lifestyle generally. It emphasizes the affective nature of exposure to a further language and culture, and recognizes that differ-ences in learning styles are inevitable and exciting.

The humanistic principles box might also be more explicitly defined:

humanistic principles	=	promoting freedom to express self recognizing the learner as resource ensuring learner freedom from authority valuing self-expression as intelligent recognizing centrality of personal discovery respecting individual learning styles

One obvious contribution of a broadly humanistic methodology to the teaching of writing is that it solves the problem of what to write about. If the information that is to be reorganized into an effective text is provided by the learner, the problem of what to write about largely disappears.

For this reason, the subject-matter of the writing exercises in Part 2 of this book is essentially learner biography, or that which learners wish to relate. In fact, we very often suggest tabulating elements from the biographies of several learners, and not necessarily in linguistic form either, to serve as the material to be written about. One frustrating element of some language-learning experiences is that one never gets to express oneself – we believe that an important part of learner motivation lies in freeing this pent-up desire.

A second contribution of a humanistic methodology to the teaching of writing lies in its recognition of the inappropriacy of offering learners models of language for them to imitate. There are good reasons for believing that a process-related approach to teaching writing is preferable to a model-offering or product-related one anyway – as we shall argue in detail in the next chapter. This is a view very strongly confirmed by humanistic principles.

The writing classroom

Although many of the ideas we have discussed so far in this introduction will be taken up subsequently, it may be helpful at this stage to give a diagrammatic characterization of what should be going on in the writing class as we see it. The diagram opposite builds on what has already been discussed in relation to communicative practice, an integrated approach and humanistic principles.

2   Writing as a deficit skill

It is not possible to learn what no one knows, and it is not necessary to learn what everyone knows. Thus teaching is about helping one group of people to do what another group can already do. This is a very simple point which is all too frequently lost sight of. But its implication is clear. Classroom time should be spent on those elements of a task that are

THE LEARNER IS CENTRAL

difficult or problematical for learners, but second nature for experts. In order to single out these elements for special attention, therefore, it must be worth asking precisely what is difficult about writing and, specifically, about writing in a second language.

We think that there are two ways of answering this question. The first way is to say that it is difficult to write a book, or a poem, or an essay. In fact, it is very difficult – why don't you try it now: just write a poem before you read the next sentence! And yet it is the approach which seems to us most typical of writing classes: to think that what has to be taught is not the step-by-step process by which a text is put together, but rather how to ape the total product of another writer. It is not an approach which appeals much in the teaching of the other skills, where the importance of a step-by-step method is generally accepted. For that reason, we would like to answer the question in a second way.

We believe it is those processes of writing that come as second nature to the expert which are difficult for the learner. They certainly include:
- organizing the information to be conveyed;
- deciding on the relative prominence to be given to any particular point;
- incorporating what one learns from listening and reading;
- expressing complex ideas appropriately;
- understanding and respecting cultural constraints;
- understanding and taking account of genres;
- knowing, and then persuading, one's readers;
- rewriting, including expressing meaning exactly and writing accurately.

If one accepts that classroom time should be spent on what is difficult or problematical for the learner, then these elements of the writing process are what one should focus on.

In practice, this step-by-step approach will mean that one focuses on particular writing skills or on particular features of good writing. Thus, for example, one exercise may focus strongly on organization, perhaps with special emphasis on classifying information or on illustrating arguments. Another may focus more on rewriting, perhaps with a special emphasis on finding the most exact expression of an intended meaning. A third may focus on respecting cultural constraints, with a particular emphasis on using sources or on questioning established views.

Finally, we return to the question of difficulty. So far in this section we have been considering writing as difficult. We believe that the more product-oriented a writing class is, the more difficult it will be for the students to write. It therefore follows that when a writing activity appears to have a lower profile, it will be easier. Thus the teacher may sometimes decide not to declare the aim of the writing class (e.g., illustrating arguments or using sources) at the outset. For this reason, we sometimes suggest a series of apparently incidental writing tasks which are not in themselves very difficult. But when completed, the learner has demonstrated the required skill or mastered the targeted feature of good writing unconsciously and relatively easily.

3   The following chapters

The major part of this book is a set of exercises which you will find in Part 2. Part 1 sets out the rationale for these classroom-tested activities each of which aims to develop a particular writing skill.

In chapter 1, we explore the nature of the writing process itself, together with the general implications of this for learning how to write. One of the elements we look at carefully in chapter 1 is the real involvement of the writer struggling to find the right form for what he or she really wants to say.

Although relatively short, chapter 2 is a particularly important part of the book. In it we explore the rather neglected field of cultural assumptions about writing. It is true that it is very often difficult to understand why a learner's writing still feels unsatisfactory when the surface problem stems from an unconsciously held erroneous view of what is required in the culture. Let us take a simple case. In some sectors of British society it is considered polite to write a short letter of thanks after having had a meal at someone's house. It is not the syntax which gives trouble so much as whether to write the letter or not, what to put in it, and what level of formality to adopt.

Chapters 3, 4 and 5 are about preparing to teach writing. They include sections on how to draw up a syllabus for a writing class, the problem of evaluating writing, and how to make the most of the 44 exercises we suggest. In order to help you with this we have dealt in chapter 5 with the practicalities of using these ideas in the classroom. You will notice that, except for plenty of paper and some means of putting work up on the wall, it is possible to set up most of the exercises without elaborate equipment or materials.

When you get to Part 2, you will see that the exercises have been grouped in categories that relate closely to the types of writing difficulty which we have already discussed. The first exercise in each category is one that should work well in almost any advanced writing class, and is also relatively simple for the teacher to organize. You may therefore want to try this one first. The remaining exercises in each category are listed alphabetically by topic. Although we discuss the criteria for selecting exercises in some detail in chapters 3 and 5, the exercises are not organized sequentially so as to constitute a course. We think that, in a teacher's resource book such as this, the order in which the materials are used should be determined by the needs and interests of each particular class, and not by us.

Finally, if you are reading this introduction and wondering whether to use this book or not, we would remind you that we concentrate on the process of writing rather than on analysing models or products. Though we believe in the value of elegant, lucid, finished products using the conventions of the genre intelligently, we also believe the teaching of writing should be open, relaxed, often collaborative, and not striving to mould itself to a model that may not, as it stands, accommodate what one really wants to say. If these ideas interest you, we invite you to read further.

1 The writing process

Before looking in detail at classroom strategies for developing the writing skills of learners, we shall put these in a broader context on the assumption that it is helpful to consider day-to-day decisions about teaching within a more general framework. So in each section of this chapter we shall look first at broad principles and then at their general implications for the teaching of writing.

1.1 Purpose

What are we doing when we write? Lloyd Jones put it this way: 'We can represent purposes in language within three rather broad but distinct categories: explanatory, persuasive, and expressive' (Frederiksen and Dominic, 1982, p. 175). A tripartite view is common in the literature and though we do not believe all writing is covered by the above three terms or indeed by our preferred terms – informing, persuading, and clarifying – such a division covers most of the major purposes of writing. We use the word informing because it has a wider scope than explanatory. A news item, for instance, is written to inform rather than explain. We use the word clarifying rather than, or in addition to, expressive as it includes more readily the writer who puts pen to paper to test whether his or her own ideas are coherent and clear. Literary writing, however, does not fall very easily into any one of these categories; nor is it easy to find a place for the friendly letter which serves largely to keep up a social contact rather than to inform, persuade, or clarify. Most writing, however, falls into one or more of the above categories. Persuading implies an audience to persuade, just as informing implies an audience that has imperfect knowledge of a subject. In either case the audience is of considerable importance. This is why we include a specific set of exercises for taking readership into account in the second half of the book. A consciousness of readership affects the way we write as well as the information we include. Our writing style, therefore, involves a sensitivity to our readers and their knowledge, beliefs, and expectations as well as being a reflection of ourselves.

   How, then, does an awareness of the purposes for which we write affect our teaching of writing in an EAP context? Within an institution, much of the writing is ostensibly to inform the teacher about facts. The paradox is that the teacher probably knows them already. In fact, the real purpose may well be for the learner to persuade the teacher that he or she has read widely, knows the topic, and can marshall facts and opinions clearly. The ostensible purpose of informing someone of something they already know may, indeed, seem a rather pointless activity from a commonsense view in the real world. One of the ways of avoiding this in the English class is to develop writing exercises that genuinely inform others of things they do not know already. A popular teaching device is the specially constructed information-gap exercise. However, we would argue strongly that it is desirable where possible for learners to write for other members of the class about interests, personal hopes, fears, beliefs, or background.

In subjects other than English, most writing tasks require the writer to inform – even though this means bridging an entirely make-believe information gap. This informing purpose means that the writer has to posit an imaginary reader with slightly eccentric gaps in knowledge.

Dissertations, on the other hand, often incorporate material new to the reader, and therefore serve to inform in a more genuine way. The writer of a dissertation also has to persuade the reader that the framework of investigation is scholarly, that the ideas expressed are original, and that any data collected is helpful.

It must be remembered that persuasion may be of two kinds. This book you are reading at the moment may, on the one hand, be trying to persuade you that a certain teaching style can be used in developing learners' writing skills. It may, on the other hand, also be persuading you actually to try one or two of the exercises to see whether they work for you. So we can persuade people to believe something or to do something. Most classroom writing is of the former kind. In the English classroom it is not difficult to create the right environment to enable the learner to express something he or she wants to persuade others about. This may be in speech or writing and often in a mixture of the two. For instance, a learner may have a very strongly held view of what constitutes real freedom and may be prepared to put those opinions on paper as an embodiment of that view. Other members of the group may argue that the original writer was wrong in substance, or that the words used could be changed to convey the intended meaning more accurately. The first learner may well wish to reply – this time in speech.

The third purpose is, as we have seen, clarifying. We may well find, for instance, that putting ideas into diagrammatic form clarifies ideas or data. Extending writing, in turn, may further clarify those ideas or possibly persuade others of the significance or relative importance of the information which has been presented in diagrammatic form. For instance, if our learners were to conduct a survey about some political issue of the moment inside and/or outside the institution, putting the results in diagrammatic form would ensure clarity of thinking and would also make the facts of the survey easily available to others. Commenting on this data would further clarify it, as well as highlighting the significance of some of the details.

Persuasion, as we mentioned earlier, is an important purpose in writing, but there are, as we have noted, other purposes and each of them affects in some measure the way we write. It is therefore important to help learners to become conscious of the purpose underlying each piece of writing. This will help them to match what they want to convey and how it is to be written.

If we compare spoken language with written, we can observe the same process of modifying the language to match the purpose. The next section explores other similarities and differences between written and spoken language.

1.2   Spoken and written language

There has been a strong belief among writers about language this century that spoken language is primary and that written language develops from it. Written language has consequently been considered to be both derivative and invariably serving separate functions. For instance, it has often been assumed that written language is necessarily formal in relation to spoken language.

However, in the past decade particularly, linguists have given a higher status to written language, showing that it has in some ways developed separately from spoken language, and they have, at the same time, demonstrated that the purposes for which spoken and written language are used are part of the culture of a society or institution rather than properties of written or spoken language. For instance, a particular society at a particular moment in time may favour almost entirely the written form for recording important information, whereas the same society at a more advanced technological stage may keep important information in a spoken form on tape. The White House at the time of Watergate was aware that information was on both, and attempts were made both to shred documents and to scrub tapes.

Just as society chooses to use primarily spoken or written language to perform a particular task even though, in theory, the task could have been fulfilled by either medium, so an educational institution will build up a tradition of which medium is used for what. For example, the British educational system tends to favour the written form whenever assessment is involved and, even where spoken assessment is introduced, it rarely carries as much weight. Similarly, in the classroom, there is often an assumption that a particular activity should be spoken rather than either written or in a mixed mode.

Let us accept that the most formal products are often written rather than spoken. Nevertheless, as Stubbs (1987) has shown, writing can be used in a number of ways that we usually think of as spoken. It can, for instance, be interactive (as in an exchange of letters), face to face (as in some communication with deaf people), have no time lapse (as in two people making up a shopping list together), and informal (as in passing simple notes while someone else is talking). This means that if we only use written language for formal work in the classroom we are not reflecting how it is used in the outside world and we are being too dogmatic in tending to assume that written language is formal and spoken informal.

Furthermore, in ordinary life written and spoken language are more interrelated than we are accustomed to thinking: we talk on the telephone and write down a message, we throw ideas around in conversation and then put them down in written form, we read bits of a letter aloud and discuss what we have read. So both in logic and in practice the spoken and the written mode share more common purposes than we sometimes realize.

The exercises in the second part of the book tend to reflect our view that the two activities can be creatively interrelated in the classroom. To illustrate the methodology let us look at one way of evaluating a course on completion. (Evaluation of this kind, however it is done, is crucial to developing professional courses that meet the learners' requirements.) The instructions to the teacher which follow are suitable for use with a class of about 30 learners:

1. Divide the class into six groups.
2. Brainstorm on the board the aspects of the course people would like to comment on.
3. Reduce these, with the aid of the learners, to six topics.
4. Give a topic to each of the six groups.
5. Each group should come to some conclusion about their topic and write the conclusion at the top of a piece of A4 paper.
6. The six pieces of paper should be attached to the wall, and individual learners asked to make comments in the space below. These may support or disagree with the group conclusions and with each other.
7. Each group rewrites their section to incorporate the views of other learners.

This is, of course, no more than a short illustration of a general principle; but it does show that a single skill such as writing can be informal at one moment (stage 6) and formal at another (stage 7), and that two skills can be combined in a single activity (speaking and writing at stage 5) with a common purpose.

The general lessons to be drawn for the classroom are, then, that we can give spoken and written language equal status, that we should not hesitate to use them for unusual purposes (such as conducting a dialogue on paper), and that we should feel free to integrate them.

When we speak, we are usually very conscious of the listeners and try to adapt our speech to their knowledge and interests. As we integrate activities, we realize that this same type of adaptation needs to happen as we tailor our writing to the knowledge and interests of the reader. The next section on readership develops this point.

1.3   Readership

One of the best ways of observing what a marked effect a consciousness of readership has on the writer is to look at the same news item in several newspapers. The writers of such articles produce very different products depending on what they consider the reading ability, the political views, and the ability to absorb abstract statements of the potential reader to be. What is not so apparent is that the writer will have a secondary readership in mind as well. This is an evaluative readership which we might call the editor/manager/censor readership. Its function is largely critical and it will be asking such questions as:
– Will this help the paper to sell?
– Will it contravene the Official Secrets Act or other regulations?
– Will it shine by the side of a competitor's article?
– Will it land the paper in an expensive libel suit?
– Is it in line with the political slant of the paper?
The writer will also have to work within the constraints of length and deadline. Clearly then the effects of both primary and secondary audience are crucial in writing.

Academic writing will have similar elements. An examination answer, for instance, whether it is a piece of writing for continuous assessment or a question in a three-hour examination, will possibly have the teacher as first reader. There will be constraints of length and timing and there will also be secondary readership in the form of the external examiner. Similarly in EAP work, the English teacher provides one kind of readership and the subject teacher another. The concept of secondary readership is possibly even clearer if we consider a particularly good piece of research which is suitable for publication. As the researcher starts writing a journal article, he or she will take into consideration the knowledge and expectations of the readership of that journal. At the same time there will be the consciousness of the secondary readership, e.g., the editor and potential reviewer. There will also be constraints of length and timing, which are of course closely related to a consciousness of the editor as secondary reader.

An awareness of the reader's previous knowledge is important even in the simplest forms of writing. When we write down a telephone message, for instance, we choose between whether to refer to a caller by first name, first and surname, or name and designation according to our judgement of how well the recipient knows the caller. This sensitivity to what a reader does or does not know is an important element in writing.

Here are two activities which you may find interesting and helpful to yourself as consciousness-raising exercises and which might equally be interesting and useful to your learners.

1. Divide a page into three vertical columns and write in these headings:

writing activity	primary readership	secondary readership

In the first column list types of writing that you do and then fill in the primary and secondary readerships, for example:

writing activity	primary readership	secondary readership
post card sent from holiday	friend who receives it	other people who may pick it up
official letter	addressee	colleagues reading file

2. Divide another sheet of paper into four columns and this time put in these headings:

primary reader group	text type	writer	secondary reader group/s

Under the four headings list the groups you belong to as a primary reader, the type of text this readership relates to, the writer/s of these texts and any individuals or groups who are secondary readers. For example:

primary reader group	text type	writer	secondary reader group/s
committee members	minutes	secretary	management
students	text books	author	publisher/critics/ teachers

The importance of taking the main possible readerships into account as you are writing is highlighted by these two activities.

The whole question of secondary readership is an important one and on the whole neglected in the literature, though it is often of considerable importance both in academic and non-academic writing. In addition to the above, it is worth considering whether one is a secondary reader oneself, even if the only answer is that someone has asked one to read a letter they have written before it is sent off!

The importance of readership is very clearly expressed in the words of Kenneth S. Goodman: 'Texts are shaped as much by the writer's sense of the characteristics of their readers as they are by the writer's own characteristics. That is as true for a shopping-list or a letter as it is for a newspaper report or a novel' (Singer and Ruddell, 1985, p. 816).

When we consider how to develop a sense of readership in the learners we are responsible for, our first thought may well be to find some way of writing for a real audience. At school level we may try to develop a pen-friend system with another institution or encourage the writing of letters to the newspapers. These projects and others like them are, however, difficult to set up or indeed to monitor, and are even harder to arrange at the tertiary level of education. They do, however, provide some practice and a reminder that writing is for real and involves taking readership into account.

But there are two interesting alternatives – for the writing done for the teacher to reflect more imaginatively the teacher as audience, and for members of a class to write for each other. So often in the classroom, writing done for the teacher tends to be bland and neutral, as if the teacher is not an interested reader so much as a corrector of mistakes. But if the language teacher first details his or her interests in the student's research area as well as what he or she does or does not know about the topic, then the student has a sharper sense of audience.

The other alternative – that of groups of learners writing for other groups in the same class – is simple to set up and highly effective, provided that the individual or group being written for is actually interested in reading the offered text. There are a number of ways in which this interest may be stimulated. As you will see from the exercises in the second half of this book, they include:
– writing for or about the member of the class who will be the reader;
– writing from information supplied by the destined reader;
– comparing data supplied by several members of the class;
– allowing the reader to change, modify, add to or even spoil the text;
– allowing the reader to call for a rewrite;
– allowing readers to combine texts with their own.
Such strategies can provide EAP teachers with interesting ideas to use with their students. The points being made here can be exemplified through many of the exercises. For example, in exercise 27 (*Comparison*

– *similarity and difference*) learners write for each other in pairs and then for the whole class.

So the first group of strategies for making the sense of readership more real to the writer is to ensure that there are opportunities for both the teacher and learners to read material of real interest.

The second group of strategies involves helping the writer to become his or her own best reader. Clearly, one strategy will be self-correction. An even more important skill is what we call 'reading in role'. This is best explained by reference to the use of improvised drama in language teaching. If learners are to act effectively using their own unscripted words, they need to know about the situation out of which the action develops and about the people they are portraying. In the same way, if the writer can build up a realistic picture of the reader's background and knowledge, he or she can then reread what has been written in role. This means that, after any particular draft of writing, the writer becomes an imaginary reader, and the draft becomes an external object. The more fully the writer is able to enter the mind of the reader he or she is postulating, the more apparent the difficulties or inadequacies of the writing. Part of the teacher's skill is choosing classroom strategies that raise the writer's awareness of the knowledge, interests, and presuppositions of the likely reader. Reading in role may be felt to be too complex a task for the second-language writer but, in fact, a sense of readership, however vague, must precede even fairly simple writing. Academic writing is certainly often flawed when students have not worked out with their teacher's help exactly what knowledge to assume on the part of the subject teacher or examiner.

It is not only the attempt to gauge the knowledge of the reader, but also the reader's perceived relationship between the writer and him or herself that is important. In a textbook, the writer may quite properly simplify the text to match the abilities (linguistic and otherwise) of the reader. In a journal article, he or she must be seen to treat the reader as an equal. In an academic assignment, the writer must be seen not to presume a relationship and to do this must use the language that signals asymmetric power relationships without being over-subservient or appearing to be hesitant. As the writer, then, reads his or her own draft in role, he or she must be aware of how the lecturer/reader views that relationship and how the language used is felt to signal that relationship. This is the kind of skill that Criper and Davies (1986) set out to test. Some examples may serve to clarify these points. For instance, if the writer is certain about something, he or she can signal their involvement in a very personal way such as 'I am sure...' or a very impersonal way 'The present author is certain...' or somewhere in-between such as 'One can be sure...'. Similarly, the reader can be included in a group of people very clearly as in 'We have all at times come across...' or less certainly as in 'Many people have at times come across...'.

There is an interesting corollary to these points. If it is important to work out and negotiate through language the role relationship between writer and reader, it becomes difficult to use one piece of writing as an exact model for another. For instance, a journal article would reflect the wrong role relationship between writer and reader if it were used as a model by a student writing an assignment. Though it is often helpful to have made decisions about format and arrangement of material beforehand, the actual writing must come from struggling to find the best words to match the writer's ideas to a particular readership rather than the straight imitation of a product, which might have been written for a different readership. This important relationship between process and product forms the basis of our next section.

1.4   Process and product

Before proceeding with this section, it may well be worth reminding ourselves of what these words mean. A product is the end result of our labours and has about it an air of finality and completeness. Process is the means by which we reach such a product. The product of another person when it serves as an example for the writer is, of course, referred to as a model.

The first point that should be made is that the distinction between process and product is not always clear cut. Sometimes there are alternative final products for different readerships. For instance, a car maintenance book about a particular model of a car will appear in one form for the trade and in another form for the ordinary motorist. Or, to take another example, first editions of academic books are often replaced by second, more scholarly editions, the changes owing much to suggestions made by reviewers and others. In this second case we may prefer to think of the second edition as an improved version of the first rather than as being addressed to a different readership. What is clear is that it is difficult to tell when a piece of writing has become an unchangeable, final product.

In almost every aspect of life the distinction between final product and draft is blurred. Take even an invitation. This may be of a standard, formal kind, but we may well add a sentence or two to family and closer friends to take into account this very different relationship.

Normally the term *draft* is used for a version of the text which the writer knows he or she will improve on. Correcting or rewriting a draft is thus a regular, and very important, part of the whole writing process. This is an aspect of writing to which we shall return.

Let us now turn to the process of writing itself. Many of the difficulties of research into the writing process (much of which comes from the United States) are related to how far the researcher can get inside the writer's mind during the process of composing. There are three standard methods, each of which has its own advantages:

Introspection – the researchers observe themselves at work writing, and afterwards note down what went on in their own minds during writing. This is difficult to do and not always objective enough.

Observation – the researcher observes and notes down all the outward signs of another writer at work – the stops and starts, the emendations, the blockages, as well as examining the completed draft.

Protocol technique – the experimental technique in which writers talk through what is going on in their minds as they make decisions about writing. This commentary is picked up by a tape-recorder, and the researchers study this afterwards to ascertain as much as they can about what was going on in the mind of the writer.

So far these techniques have been used mainly with semi-professional writers writing in their first language but the results may well have more general relevance. Although each technique has limitations, in combination they give us a good deal of insight into what actually goes on as we write. The findings clearly have considerable relevance for what goes on in the classroom, although it is not clear how much they help with the really unpractised and immature writer. Beach and Bridwell (1984, p. 127) describe what has become something of a consensus among researchers:

> The most important development in composition research over the
> last decade has been the study of the composing process: the ways
> writers discover ideas, formulate goals and plans, express their ideas,
> assess their own writing, revise, and edit.

They also mention categories already current in the literature such as *reformulating*, *stopping*, *reflecting*, and *changing*.

Many researchers are at pains to point out that often these processes go on side by side or are interwoven and cannot be thought of as forming some kind of tidy linear progression. For instance, not all ideas are generated before writing begins, indeed, the act of writing often sparks off new ideas.

Furthermore, all writers have to generate ideas, put these into words internally, and then find the correct written form in which to get them on to paper. The short-term memory is put under particular strain as writers in a second language find the syntax and vocabulary to encapsulate their ideas and then struggle to get these down on paper in the correct form.

23

This makes it much harder to maintain a coherent train of thought, though it can be considerably helped by clear decisions about how to organize and arrange the material.

Perhaps the most important lesson to be learned from our examination of the writing process is that much writing outside the classroom is often casual and relaxed. Whether it is an *aide memoire* for ourselves, a telephone message, or a friendly letter, we normally do not strain to create a perfect final product. Furthermore, if we are writing in a second language outside the classroom, we tend to use the language at our disposal to make ourselves understood. If, therefore, we want to make writing in the classroom more like what happens in the outside world, it becomes important to build an atmosphere there that considers writing to be an ordinary task, not beset by anxiety, and one which makes use of the language at the learner's disposal as effectively as possible.

There are many ways in which this natural and anxiety-free use of written language can be built into classroom activities. For instance, when a group of learners first meets, one way of introducing learners to each other is to ask each in turn to mention characteristics, personal interests, and details about themselves but without giving their names. Each member of the class then moves around freely, talking to each other person in turn and, having successfully matched the person to one of the sets of characteristics previously written down, asks and records his or her name. One result of this activity is to begin to work towards a trusting and open classroom where each person is thought of and valued for themselves. This process activity shows how easy, natural, and meaningful writing in the classroom can be.

We would like to suggest one more class activity which is also casual and carries minimal stress. It is an activity that is typically treated as a speaking or listening exercise and as such does not completely fall within the scope of the exercises at the end of the book. However, it may prove useful at this point to demonstrate the way communicative speaking activities can be extended to include writing of an informal kind.

Take the well-known ice-breaker where learners position themselves on an imaginary clock-face at the hour of the day when they feel their best. Typically, they are asked to discuss the similarities between themselves and the other people who have chosen the same hour, and then share these discoveries orally with the rest of the class. This can be transformed into primarily a writing task by asking each other group to write a profile for themselves in the form: 'X o'clock people are people who ... They make excellent ...' These profiles are then read aloud while the other groups make brief notes. Finally, each group composes a proposal to another group explaining why the two groups are compatible, what is attractive about the other group's lifestyle, and suggesting they get together.

In simple ways like this, writing can become both more natural and more easily integrated in language learning activities. This is an indication of how speaking/listening activities in a notional/functional or communicative coursebook can be translated into written ones.

Another important element in the process of writing, which appears first on the list in the Beach and Bridwell passage quoted earlier in this section, is discovering ideas. We can plan for this and for the related element of formulating goals and plans through initial discussion in groups or through some discussion after preliminary writing. However, we will not fall into the trap of thinking that we have to move in an orderly fashion from getting ideas, to organizing them, to writing them down. We will allow for the fact that, as we write, we wish to change things, to discuss them, to reorder our material, to make things sound more elegant. So we will build in discussion not only at the start but in the course of writing too.

Another element of the process of writing is assessing the accuracy and effectiveness of one's own writing, and reformulating it. It is worth noting that in a recent article Anne Chenoweth argued that this reformulation is characteristic of expert rather than poor writers.

When learners are unable to reformulate their own work satisfactorily, the EAP teacher may, in the most favourable circumstances, work alongside them helping them to do so. This is, however, not often possible in practice. So another strategy is to take the work of one or two students and reformulate it for use with the whole class, by having it photocopied and used for class discussion. This can be a useful technique but it has some major drawbacks. For instance, the topic and technical language of the piece chosen may prove difficult or off-putting for others in the class. Furthermore, the problems thrown up for discussion by the piece may not be those facing the bulk of the learners. The optimum time to give assistance is when the writer is struggling to express a particular meaning, or considering the best form of phrasing, or puzzling over some convention. By breaking up the tasks and building in peer discussion, the provision of help in an unthreatening way at the point of need is so much more effective. Even where it is not possible to provide help at the moment of greatest need, activities can be designed which facilitate working co-operatively towards a solution to typical problems. There must be many teachers, for instance, who have thought about how to deal effectively with 'I' when it is used inappropriately in a piece of formal work. How can the teacher encourage the correct use of the tentative 'I' and discourage the use of non-standard 'I' to signal important generalities? Rather than correct wrong usages in a completed piece of work, how much better it would be to get our learners to use 'I' in an acceptable way, naturally, in a class activity that held interest. Having learned to do it once enjoyably, our learners have the facility to use it in further writing (see exercise 14, *'I' in formal writing*).

Another point that a study of process reminds us of is that we must find some way of helping our learners as they struggle to complete a sentence which is giving them problems. It is only too easy to set up rather dull, behaviouristic sentence-completion exercises as an attempt to meet this point. However, if we decide to start a series of sentences in such a way that a learner would want to complete them in a meaningful way and that a fellow-learner would want to respond to them, we would be setting up an exercise that would specially help a second-language learner. It is particularly helpful to work at meaningful sentence completion because of the difficulty of keeping long sentences in mind while sorting out sense, syntax, vocabulary, and the process of writing down – a point referred to earlier in this section. For instance, after beginnings such as 'Would you tell a lie if . . . ?' it is natural to want to finish the question. There would be considerable interest in how it was completed as well as in a fellow-learner's answer!

Finally, the process of writing is to do with the solving of many interrelated microproblems and so it is important to try to identify what these are. There is no easy answer to this, but really professional teachers will observe their own writing processes as well as those of the learners and will discuss the problem areas with them. We have done this in our own work (which we have described earlier) and the observations made have become the focuses of the activities in the second part of this book. The problems we have identified are common to many learners who have embarked on academic writing courses. However, needs differ slightly with different classes and you may care to use the focuses we identify as a starting-point for drawing up your own modified list.

One of the interesting points that emerges when one stands back and looks at the writing process – as has been done in this section – is that one's own best practices are confirmed and given a rationale. At the same time, we may all be led to rethink some of the things we have typically done in the writing class, and this may well lead to the development of new teaching strategies.

1.5   Genre analysis

One of the most influential concepts behind accepted methodology for teaching English for Academic Purposes in the 1980s has been the analysis of *genres*. Because there are various stages in the theoretical and pedagogic arguments, we will look first at what is self-evident to the layperson, and then at some of the aspects of genre analysis found in the theoretical literature. We also consider what the consequences for work in the classroom appear to be according to the pedagogical literature (which is sometimes conflated with the theoretical arguments). Finally, we discuss the usefulness or otherwise of these ideas in practice.

There is little doubt that the layperson understands the existence and something of the nature of different genres. It is, for instance, not difficult to distinguish between an advertisement for a house and a surveyor's report on it, even though they are basically describing the same object. The purpose of the description is different and this has an effect on the selection and ordering of the facts, their relative prominence, and the kind of language used to describe them.

Learned articles or doctoral theses within a particular discipline are good examples of a genre and much of the theoretical work done in this area has been on such materials, e.g., Swales (1981) and Dudley-Evans (1986). The latter defines a genre as follows:

A genre is a more or less standardized communicative event with a
goal or set of goals mutually understood by the participants in that
event, and occurring within a functional rather than social or
personal setting.

He goes on to show how academic genres have favoured *moves* (parts) and have such parts in a favoured order. He quotes Swales (1981) as showing that the introductions to scientific journal articles consist of the following moves:
— establishing the field;
— summarizing previous research;
— preparing for present research;
— introducing present research.
But a careful reading of writers such as Swales demonstrates that he is much less dogmatic about the occurrence or ordering of the different elements than at first appears. His is very much a descriptive and analytical approach. Furthermore, on every occasion where one of the early writers on genre analysis showed any tendency to be dogmatic, counter-examples were cited in the literature. It became clear that there were observable tendencies and regularities rather than strict rules. Certain elements always appear somewhere in a piece of writing either by necessity or by regulation (e.g., some institutions insist on an initial abstract in thesis writing). These we can call 'mandatory constraints'. A far larger number of non-mandatory elements appear in most examples of a genre, and, although they help to define it as a genre, they may be omitted or shifted around for particular purposes. These we can call

'customary constraints'. Finally, there are elements that can be included or omitted at will, which can be called 'open options'.

One way of analysing texts in order to regularize and simplify such an analysis is to search for underlying functions. One set which has long been current in the literature and is helpfully referred to by Hamp-Lyons and Heasley (1987, p. 100) is *situation – problem – solution – evaluation*. Being able to talk about a piece of writing in such general terms is clearly useful both for the teacher and the learner since it gives an indication of its likely structure.

The next point we want to make is that the particular realization of a given function will allow considerable variation. This can be simply illustrated from the writing of business letters. Many business letters start with a reference to previous communication and to the general topic of the letter. These functions can be realized by sentences such as: 'Thank you for your letter of April 25. We are now in a position to give you more information...' It is often helpful to talk about these and other elements of a business letter considering whether they are required and if there is an accepted order before separately looking at alternative ways of expressing them. This separation of elements or functions within a text from their realizations in language is an important contribution of genre analysis to teaching about text.

Let us consider next the stages at which genre analysis is genuinely useful and then separately look at its limitations and dangers. In the first place, it is a useful tool for analysing texts. It is worth exploring how it may help at the very early stages of reading within a subject area that the learner will later be writing in. There is little doubt that what we read has a considerable effect on what and how we write. The more thoughtfully and discriminatingly we read, the more likely it is to have a direct and conscious effect on our writing. For this reason, where an academic assignment or thesis is the end-product, the reading of academic assignments and theses as well as books and journal articles will be important. The favoured terminology and syntactic choices will start to influence us, as will the general structure of the work. Genre analysis will enable the reader to analyse the structure more effectively and therefore to be more conscious of it while reading.

The second stage is the immediate planning stage. The learner embarking on a major piece of work feels cautious about writing sections of it till he or she has thought more about the general plan of the work. The results of genre analysis allow the writer to consider what elements are expected in the writing of a particular genre and what their customary order is. He or she can then consider what to omit or add and what order to put the elements in. It is particularly relevant when the learner is writing instrumentally, and is more anxious about fulfilling requirements than expressing new ideas.

The third stage is the draft stage. Writers, by considering the overall shape of the draft they have written, are able to make more meaningful changes than if they look only at the surface features. The sense of overall shape developed by genre analysis helps by causing writers to consider deleting, expanding or changing the order of complete sections of the text as well as making minor corrections to individual sentences.

To turn now to the limitations and dangers of being too dependent on genre analysis, let us consider writers who have something new to say – perhaps as the result of unexpected laboratory results. A predetermined framework may not permit such writers to make the new points as efficiently and in as balanced a way as they could wish. If there is too much of a mismatch between the requirements of the genre and what needs to be said, such writers may even find it difficult to think as clearly as they should. This will be because they are trying to fit their ideas into a mould that was actually designed for a different situation. It is also true that many writers are inhibited in struggling towards the best structure for their writing by sensing that there is a predetermined pattern they are required to fit into.

We must conclude that there is a paradox here. For some learners, at some point, it is important to look at the structure of written work as a whole. For this, genre analysis may be of help and we suggest reading some of the good literature on the subject listed in the bibliography. For ourselves, we are committed to allowing the form to develop from the struggle to express meaning, and the general thrust of this book is in this direction. We do recognize the value of genre analysis, however, and particularly the fact that because it is concerned with the content of different moves it is possible to talk about ideas and their possible deployment rather than strictly following a model. It is particularly important that the analysis of text-types remains descriptive rather than (as it has sometimes become) prescriptive, and that it does not make the writer forget either his or her intended message or his or her reader.

To sum up, if each move is thought of as a meaning counter to be shuffled into the order that best suits the writer's purposes rather than the lecturer's preconceptions, genre analysis can be an excellent servant instead of a somewhat restrictive master.

2 Cultural assumptions about writing

2.1 The nature of the problem

This chapter deals with a problem that most of us who teach writing are worried by. The exact nature of the problem is not easy to identify, and even harder to remedy. Apart from one or two honourable exceptions, it has received little satisfactory treatment in the literature. We are, of course, referring to underlying assumptions about the nature of academic disciplines, the way in which work in those disciplines is presented in writing, the supposed insider audience, their knowledge and expectations, and the whole sense of how to relate the new piece of writing to what has been written before. Sometimes the term *contrastive rhetoric* is used to describe at least part of what we have been considering, although the issue is broader than that.

The problem typically presents itself when we come across a piece of writing that is apparently correct in its surface features. There may be the odd sentence that, though it is grammatical, sounds unnatural because of wrong ordering or unusual collocations. Having allowed for that, there is still something exotic about the text. Very often we find that it is in the ordering of the material, the treatment of previous writers, or the degree (or otherwise!) of tentativeness that cause the piece of writing to seem to belong to another culture.

Our first task may well be to identify the mismatch between cultures or genres. Our second task is to decide what to do about it. If we decide to tackle the problem at all, the first stage is to examine whether our suggestions for change are the result of our own cultural imperialism – a term used by Philip Riley, who also stresses that we need to consider carefully before imposing our own cultural assumptions on our learners. The second stage – crucial for this book, for instance – is what strategies to adopt if we are helping learners to match their cultural assumptions to those of the users of the language they are writing in.

The same type of problem exists with speech. In a BBC programme some years ago called *Crosstalk*, an Asian now living in Britain was making a transaction in the bank. His English was perfectly grammatical and clear, but the loudness of his voice, the stress patterns, and the difference in discourse expectations made a fundamentally polite man appear rude to the bank clerk. As with writing, there are two possible answers. The first is that the listener could well do with being educated to understand the cultural differences. The second is that the speaker should work on such things as stress patterns and loudness of voice. Similarly in the written mode, the writer would expect to try to ensure that the ordering of material and comments on other writers are matched with the culture of the target language.

These issues will be addressed directly in section 2.5, but before this we shall examine in the next section the evidence of the supposed differences in writing cultures including whether those differences extend to scientific writing. This will be followed in sections 2.3 and 2.4 by looking at how a writer's work, however humble, relates to previous writing and at what it means to be an outsider and an insider as a writer.

2.2 Which community does a writer belong to?

Through our own reading we absorb a great deal about the culture in which the texts are embedded. We acquire a sense of the underlying values and ways of thinking, of what is acceptable to put into writing and which form it should take, and of how written material is organized. This process is assisted by reading the work of other learners within our own educational institution. Such knowledge is often not conscious though it can be (and sometimes is) brought to consciousness. Whether it is or not, it often underlies our own writing in our first language.

When, however, we are called upon to write in another language we may see our task as recoding, in the same way, with the same underlying assumptions, the ideas we originally expressed in our first language. This will be particularly true if most of the reading has been in the first language, but, even if most of the reading underlying a particular piece of writing is in the second language, general cultural assumptions will still have an influence. A short list of the likelihood of a mismatch follows, starting with the greatest likelihood of mismatch and ending up with the least likelihood:
- the two written cultures are very different;
- none of the specialized reading has been done in the second language;
- some of the specialized reading has been done in the second language;
- all of the specialized reading has been done in the second language;
- much general reading has been done in the second language;
- the culture of the second language is viewed very favourably.

When a writer views the culture of a second language particularly favourably he or she seeks to become an insider in a new writing community, and this choice of writing community is a topic we will return to in section 4 of this chapter. It is important to establish first whether this perception that writing grows out of and reflects different cultures is a sound one.

The first thing to be said is that there have been a number of reports in the literature of teachers who have been able to place fairly accurately the nationality of writers of anonymous assignments. Robert Kaplan mentions this phenomenon in an early article, and this alerted him to the area of writing which he calls contrastive rhetoric. He defines the term in this way:

> My topic is contrastive rhetoric; that is, I am concerned with the notion that speakers of different languages use different devices to present information, to establish the relationship among ideas, to show the centrality of one idea as opposed to another, to select the most effective means of presentation.

Eleven years earlier he had compared English paragraph structure, which he considered to be linear, with the following types: parallel, circular, digressing and complex, which he associated with generic language types (Semitic, Oriental, Romance, Russian). Kaplan's central ideas are still widely accepted though the particularity of his work on paragraph structure has been challenged. In a recent very full survey of the field Purves (1987) raises such points as the following:
— the importance of 'writing through composing for the purpose of reporting'; this 'writing act' requires special strategies;
— that there exist 'a set of text conventions that the student is expected to be able to manage';
— the existence of both writer-responsible cultures like the British and reader-responsible cultures like the Japanese;
— the need to teach the target form and the ideological process through which one arrives at that form;
— that composition is a product arrived at through a process and that the new process must be taught as well as the new product;
— 'the fact that a student understands audience in one language system does not mean that the student understands audience in any language system'.

The concept of contrastive rhetoric has been supported by a number of other writers. Odile Regent, for instance, in writing about medical articles in English and French shows that both the underlying mindset, the written product, and its form on the page are different. She details it in this way (Riley, ed. 1985):

> For the French writers it is the scientific facts which have to be communicated, and the whole of the discourse is organized around the data to be presented. The line of argument, if it exists at all, is

secondary. In English, on the other hand, it is precisely the line of argument which is of prime importance.

Michael Clyne (Smith, 1987) demonstrates that there are comparable differences between German and English academic writing, the latter paying greater attention to the importance of relevance and lack of repetition. Similarly, Maggie Jo St John, in a recent article, comments that Spanish academics find the over-explicitness of British writing somewhat ridiculous.

The apparent conclusion of a study of contrastive rhetoric would seem to be that the learner writing in a second language should be taught to understand the thought processes and to study the written products, including the formal conventions of writing, in the target language. Is this the only conclusion to be drawn from the work of Kaplan and others?

The first point to make is that it is only too easy to become what Philip Riley would term a cultural imperialist. It is possibly somewhat arrogant and ethnocentric, for instance, to think that Spanish learners are invariably wrong not to be more explicit in their writing though if they want to satisfy assessors within the British system they will need to be so. Some British writing might, indeed, benefit from influence in the other direction. One must never forget instrumental needs and considerations, however, and when it is best simply to adopt British norms. Indeed, how one deals with cross-cultural mismatches of this kind depends largely on the purpose of the writing and the intended audience.

These issues are sharper if one turns one's attention to some British ex-colonial territories where changes in rhetorical patterns may well follow the growing acceptance of local forms of spoken English. Kachru (1986) makes this point very clearly:

[Various linguistic devices] are organized into what speakers of South Asian English consider appropriate rhetorical styles. Appropriateness is determined by several factors, the native literary and cultural traditions being very important. Above all, the notion of a proper style in a particular context is derived from languages such as Sanskrit, Persian and Arabic. In all these languages, stylistic embellishment is highly valued. These 'native' rhetorical styles are then imposed on an 'alien' language which results in functional and communicative varieties in South Asian English distinct from other Englishes.

Clearly, it is even more problematical whether to impose British norms on those who are accustomed to writing in a variety of English that has quite other features.

Another reason for not accepting the apparent solutions of contrastive rhetoric studies without question is the claim that has been made for the

universality of scientific thought and discourse. We find quite a widely
held view in the literature that scientists have a common body of
knowledge and way of looking at the world and that the main task of a
writer from another culture writing in English is virtually that they need
do no more than translate directly from one language into another. This,
too, is the view of many ESL students – a finding confirmed by a survey
carried out by Philip Shaw in Newcastle and reported on at the
SELMOUS conference in 1987:

> I wondered whether the students would feel that the conventions of
> British academic writing were different from those that prevailed in
> their own culture ... If contrastive rhetoric does present problems
> these are not recognised; the interviewees regard science as a universal
> enterprise.

It will certainly be true that in any culture there may be more difference
between writing in the arts and in the sciences than between any two
cultures in a particular scientific field, but the Regent and Clyne studies
already quoted should remind us that there are cultural differences, even
in the sciences.

A further challenge comes from the very particular studies undertaken
by Dudley-Evans and others. One recent study looks at the expectations
of the supervisors of plant biology theses at Birmingham University. We
are no longer dealing so much with contrastive rhetoric but with what
has been called *institutional-based discourse*. By adopting the norms of
an institution and of a particular discipline of that institution and of a
particular genre within that discipline, the question of cultural mismatch
at national level must recede in importance.

Nevertheless, the whole area of contrastive rhetoric is more important
than has been generally recognized and a consciousness of the kind of
differences between societies can be of great importance to teachers. They
can then decide how far to respect the existing traditions of their learners
and how far to modify them to be in line with British norms, especially
when they are the norms of those who will be assessing the work.

2.3   Entering a writing community: relating to previous writing

When Shakespeare wrote *The Merchant of Venice*, what he wrote was
partly determined by what had been written before and in turn it will
have had an influence on what he and others wrote later. In this particular
case, there was a very strong link between that play and Marlowe's *The
Jew of Malta*. *The Merchant of Venice* borrowed many ideas from *The*

Jew of Malta, improving and indirectly commenting on them. Nowadays, that kind of relationship between texts is less common. What is clear is that every text has had to take other texts into account, and the way this is done differs from culture to culture.

It may be useful to take as an example a typical publishing situation in our times. A new biography of a famous figure, for instance, is likely to be one of the following: a short readable account omitting much material from an existing biography, an account of the life from a consciously different perspective from that of a previous biography, or an extended volume to take in all the information from the latest scholarship.

Another example is that, within a higher educational institution, the title of a thesis and the thesis itself will have resulted from a careful examination of the literature on the subject both generally and within the institution. The thesis will take a good deal of trouble to review the existing literature and then to find something new to say. A thesis title will rarely if ever be repeated within its own institution. So the writer of a thesis does not have a free hand. He or she will have had to take other writing into account – both noting accepted formats and styles and also trying not to repeat or copy what has been written.

Pugsley (1988) has this to say on the related topic of what she calls 'possessability' of a text:

The area in which non-native speakers seem most unaware (or made least aware) of the inadequacy of their linguistic output is perhaps the piece of extended academic writing: tutors may be critical of the students' lack of organization of material, and apparent disregard for differentiation between straightforward plagiarism, adulterated plagiarism, relating other writers' views without critical comment and expression of own personal views. While many of these criticisms are not unjustified, the critics would seem to be approving a single 'correct' approach to the concept of ownership of the written word and the 'possessability' of text – a concept which in our own society is surely founded not only on a philosophical basis but against the highly structured background of the publishing world, on the one hand, and the attainment of academic status through one's publications on the other.

As Pugsley implies, a particular point of cultural difference in this area in general is the attitude to authority on the part of writers. Some cultures expect the learner to seek out those authorities with the highest status and to summarize, quote, and report on their main ideas. Other cultures or writing communities expect learners to challenge authority in however marginal and deferential a way. Indeed, the manner in which such a challenge is worded is also culturally determined. In British writing one of the favourite ways of challenging accepted authority is to quote contrary opinions from another writer. When a direct challenge is necessary it is often worded as impersonally as possible and even then there is a measure of tentativeness and a tendency to use caveats. We provide an exercise relating to the latter in the second half of the book (see exercise 12, *Entering caveats*). Notwithstanding all this, a challenge is expected, and this differentiates British writing from that of some academic communities elsewhere in the world.

One of the most delicate and difficult matters in this whole area is to determine the way in which what we write relates to other writing. Is our humble thesis of sufficient stature to stand by others in the field? If we write an article for publication, which journal do we send it to? Are we presumptuous if we send it to journal A? Does it say sufficient new things to be of above standard length? In ordinary life, are we presumptuous in taking the initiative in sending a letter to someone important or should we wait for them to write to us first?

What is clear is that, whether we like it or not, the moment we write we are part of a writing community. The next section will explore the question of whether we do it as insiders or as outsiders.

2.4   Insiders, outsiders and power relationships

Overseas students at a British university may be made to feel outsiders in that particular academic community. They may nevertheless know that within another academic community they are insiders. There is then both a dilemma and a choice. The dilemma is in how to resolve the tension of needing to belong to two communities and the choice is whether to become as far as possible a fully-fledged member of the new community or to refuse to change completely. Often self-identity clashes with instrumental needs such as acquiring qualifications in the new community.

What does it mean to be an insider in a particular writing community? Clearly an important aspect is to understand the assumptions that lie behind the writing and to show that one is aware of the conventions of that community and that, like other writers, one shares a knowledge of the literature. There is a second dimension to the way in which any of us belong to a writing community – that is the dimension of asymmetric power relationships. We can be an insider and equal, but also an insider and unequal. In fact, if we are too presumptuous in claiming equality when we are not being granted that status, we may find ourselves not being accepted as an insider at all.

There are linguistic ways of signalling insider status. The use of personal pronouns (the choice between 'I', 'we', or 'you', for instance) may signal membership or non-membership quite distinctly. In the same way, there are ways of signalling power relationships. To take one example, a student writing for an examiner needs to employ a measure of tentativeness, while at the same time conveying that this comes from modesty rather than uncertainty and lack of confidence.

However, not everyone wishes to be an insider. Sometimes it is a positive benefit to signal one's outsider status. For instance, psychology, sociology, or linguistics may throw interesting light on a literary text. The sociologist writing on John Donne and the particular social circumstances that made the private circulation of passionate or risqué poems possible and acceptable in Elizabethan England may prefer as he writes for literary enthusiasts to signal outsider status by using vocabulary and rhetorical ordering more usual in sociological than in literary texts. For a student, the two most likely reasons for remaining an outsider are to retain one's separate identity and culture or to avoid being thought an insider who has not quite made the grade.

Linguistically, one of the ways we can signal insider or outsider status is by the use of the definite article. Let us take an example. In discussing the focus of exercise 15 (*Promoting nominal style*), we remark on the easily verifiable fact that non-native speakers tend to use 'a/an' in the opening sentences of their writing in places where a native speaker would prefer 'the'. We think that this is a very significant fact indeed and that the explanation lies more in sociology than linguistics.

When we use the word 'the', we typically intend the reader or hearer to understand that we are referring to something known to both parties – for example, there is a presupposition that 'the children' always refers to the same two, three, four, or even classful of children, known to speaker and hearer. Similarly, in the preceding sentence, we decided to take the existence of '*the* hearer or reader' as presupposed, although, in fact, we might equally grammatically have written 'we typically intend *a* reader or hearer . . .' Why did we do this?

When we write 'we typically intend *the* reader or hearer', we expect you in some unconscious way to nod to yourself and murmur, 'Yes, I know what they mean'. Or, put another way, '*the* hearer or reader' refers to something known or given. Thus the function of noun phrases introduced (determined) by 'the' is to refer to what is known – to what can be accepted without question.

So it is not entirely surprising that if we feel ourselves to be native members of the culture, insiders in fact, we take it for granted that we and our readers have a good deal in common. And we tend to mark this common knowledge in our choice of the definite article.

37

2.5   Implications for teaching

It is vitally important that the teacher is aware that cultural mismatch, particularly in the area of rhetorical arrangement, is more than likely. It is even more important that he or she realizes that this is a mismatch and not a mistake. The learner will respond very positively to a teacher who is interested in and values the writing culture of the mother tongue. Part of respect for the learner is analysing the problem carefully and professionally and then being open with the learner. All the consequences of different courses of action need to be spelled out. For instance, it is important that learners are made aware of the effect on evaluation where a culture/language mismatch is retained in their writing.

Furthermore, the teacher must take nothing for granted. At a simple level one presumes that in every writing system letters are of comparable size, slope the same way, rest on the line, and are clear rather than decorated. In some cultures none of these things is true and the English assessor may literally or subconsciously downgrade work where handwriting looks childish even though it is following a different set of norms and ideals. One strategy must surely be to bring to consciousness what are unconscious assumptions on the part of students. In that way mismatches can be rationally dealt with.

What is equally important is to identify the micro-problems, any or all of which may give rise to a mismatch. This allows us as teachers to deal with these at the rate of perhaps one per lesson.

Take, for instance, the set of problems or difficulties that face the writer who refers to another text or to other texts. They include:
- how much to quote;
- how long the quotations should be;
- how they are integrated into the text;
- how they are acknowledged;
- how the thoughts of a writer are summarized where he or she is not being directly quoted;
- how that is acknowledged;
- how much to evaluate the thoughts of 'experts';
- whether to do so in the first person.

Whilst to your learners reference to other texts may seem a single area, to you as teacher this area raises a whole set of small but important issues.

It is important for your relationship with your learners that you are clear but not dogmatic. For instance, there are two or three generally approved ways of referencing quotations. It is worth finding out the norm in the institution and possibly showing one or two other ways of doing it, while recommending the institutional norm.

There would be a danger in using the 'instructor mode' all the time. If one is able to explore, experiment, share expertise, try things out in active and real situations, then the learners will lower their barriers and become more involved. So much is then being worked at interestingly and less consciously, that from time to time it may be important to overtly take stock of what has been discovered.

One is not so much making a frontal attack on cultural mismatch as enabling learning to take place in a way that would actually be helpful to both native and non-native speaker.

The same learner-centred techniques can be used for those organizational and linguistic skills which are to some degree culture specific. Take the linguistic skill of writing in a nominal style. As is generally recognized, this produces greater formality and is usually associated with the written mode, just as verbal style is associated with informality and the spoken mode. Both styles can, however, be used in writing. A simple example may demonstrate their rather different effects: 'The newspaper reported that Dr Jones approved of the fact that the hens were producing eggs while ranging freely' (verbal style), and 'The newspaper reported Dr Jones' approval of free-range egg production' (nominal style). Learners can be assisted in discovering the relationship between the nominal and verbal style and can learn to gauge the likely effect of each on the reader. However, the final decision as to which to use in a particular piece of writing is part of the individual writer's choice.

There is a third type of more general skill which we have termed 'the sociology of writing', implying by this term that there are cultural differences between groups speaking different languages or even the same language. One example is the way in which counter-evidence is admitted to or omitted from a piece of writing, including whether it is placed before or after the positive evidence. The British seem to differ from the members of most other cultures in preferring to place first a weak form of counter-evidence followed by as strong a presentation of positive evidence as possible.

It is apparent then that cultural mismatch may be on the organizational level (e.g., how to order different elements), on the linguistic level (e.g., whether to use nominal or verbal style), or on the general level (e.g., what to do about counter-evidence).

Finally, it is worth reminding ourselves of Kaplan's view that to be really successful, the teacher and learners together should explore the assumptions, ideologies, and views on which their writing is based and work at these and at the whole process of writing and not just at the final product.

3 Improving writing skills

If we agree that the learner is central in a writing course, certain consequences follow. Firstly, the teacher will become aware that the real purpose of the course will be to enable the learning of writing to take place. This gives teachers a different but no less important role. They become much more enablers at the process stage and much less assessors of the finished product. How does this work out in practice? We make a number of points in the sections which follow and, at the risk of covering ground which you may well be aware of ready, we describe in some detail the tasks involved in drawing up and implementing a writing programme.

3.1 Negotiating a writing programme

The learner has to believe in what he or she is doing to get the best out of any course. It is generally recognized that a readiness on the part of the teacher to listen and change a potential programme in the light of a strongly felt need is important. Equally important is a full discussion between the teacher and learners of a potential programme to demonstrate its interest, its relevance, and its good use of time. What is not possible at this level is to change the whole context of a course. For instance, in the institution in which we work, it is not part of our remit to proof-read dissertations. So when one of our students said to us, 'I am only interested in coming to this class if you help me in detail with my dissertation', we were ready to talk through reasonable alternatives, but he did not move from his initial position, and so we were forced to part. With the rest of the class, however, we were able to discuss some aspect of the dissertations or assignments of everyone in the group, and to deal with them through one or other of the exercises, but never on a one-to-one proof-reading basis. Our experience is not unique. Even when the constraints on what teachers may or may not do are strict, they can still fulfil very many individual needs within a negotiated programme.

One way of negotiating a writing programme that we have found effective is to negotiate it through a writing exercise. If, for example, each learner in the group lists his or her writing needs, and the problems he or she encounters in writing, then this naturally leads to work on classifying, ordering and summarizing. And the written outcome might serve as a menu for the first few sessions of the course. This idea has worked well with our classes, and so we suggest three writing exercises in Part 2, which have the dual aims of practising a writing skill and negotiating a writing programme (see exercises 1, 2 and 3).

We believe it is part of a proper respect for and partnership with one's learners to listen, discuss, and negotiate, and to be prepared to make changes when they will clearly benefit the class as a whole. There are two directions in which it is possible to be more radical than we are suggesting here. The first is to negotiate a syllabus by majority vote, although perhaps this sort of choice should come at the which-class-to-attend level rather than cause an unwilling minority to have to concur with the majority decision. The second is to allow each student to develop an autonomous programme. Elements of this approach seem sensible, even though it is not usually possible to go all the way down such a path. A reasonable compromise might be for an EAP department to keep short programmes available in worksheet, textbook, or computer form to cover particular points (such as connectives), the learner then being free to supplement the common course from these sources. Because we believe learners have so much to give each other, we favour a certain amount of collaborative writing which can only be done in class or group mode. The importance of having a wide range of topics and ways of dealing with them is illustrated by the case of a Korean Ph.D. student who was particularly helped by the session on arrangement of material (see exercise 25, *Selection, prominence and ordering*). Although fellow-students found topics such as cohesion and practising nominal style more helpful, they nevertheless agreed that they had benefited from this session too. This showed how a widely-based course is personally useful to all students and likely to meet the different particular needs of each individual at some stage.

3.2 Making a profile of the learner's abilities and needs

In a pronunciation programme which we also run, we ask students individually what problems they are aware of in their own speech. One student said, 'We expect you to tell us. You're the expert.' In fact, in his case it was quite possible to pick out problems of word stress and phrasing that crucially hindered intelligibility. Another student, however, was much more sure of his own problems, 'Ends of words – especially s's and t's'.

It is easy to understand that the former student should expect us to tell him about his problems rather than vice versa. Nevertheless, a balanced profile of a learner's needs and abilities will also depend on the infor-

41

mation the learner supplies. Thus, in a writing programme, it is helpful to have not only samples of written work for tutor assessment but also a degree of insight into the learners' own perceptions of their strengths and weaknesses. Both kinds of information are useful in putting together an effective programme. For this reason, one of the three exercises on negotiating a writing programme is aimed particularly at discovering learner perceptions of ability and need within the areas that the main body of the exercises focus on (see exercise 2, *Profiling learner ability and need*).

In this exercise each learner is asked to assess his or her writing needs from a checklist which includes areas such as *organizing ideas, taking the reader into account* and *accurate writing.* One of the key points in the approach we are using is to build on the interests, knowledge, language and skills that the learner already has and so the second checklist requires the learners to analyse their ability in a range of writing skills.

Once completed, the needs checklist and the abilities checklist serve several purposes. They constitute a data base that is useful to the teacher because it reveals the needs and abilities of the class and useful to the students as the basis of a writing activity in which each student compares his or her needs and abilities with those of colleagues.

The completed checklists also enable teacher and students to draw up a negotiated syllabus for the first few weeks of the writing course. Imagine, for example, that there is general agreement that the class needs to work on organizing ideas: next, the student ability levels in the three areas of checklist 2 that relate to organization (*linking paragraphs, illustrating arguments* and *making generalizations*) will give some indication of where the course might start. (Although it is clear that there are also many aspects of organization in writing other than the three indicated in checklist 2.)

We believe that, with methods like these, it is possible to reach a consensus with students on course content and at the same time to encourage learner self-awareness and self-monitoring. Thus making a profile of learner need and ability can be a positive exercise as well as a necessary one.

3.3   Targeting skills

There are those who believe that the best way to get better at writing is to write. As with most skills, practice is important, but it may result in repetitive activity for its own sake. And it is also very obviously the case that it is not only practice that is important. This is why writing classes tend to focus on writing types, or, in the case of this book, on sub-skills within the areas of difficulty discussed at the end of the introduction.

But having made the decision to work in this way, a second question arises: should learners concentrate on each targeted skill within the context of their global writing or in separate specific exercises?

We have taken the decision to work with separate exercises. Whilst it could be forcefully argued that a holistic approach gives an overview as well as an integrated grasp of the writing type required, there are at least three strong reasons for choosing separate exercises:

1. Practicality – in the typical lesson time available, one is much more likely to make real progress by targeting a sub-skill through an exercise than by picking it out of a longer passage of student writing.
2. Face validity – in a negotiated programme that is responsive to learner need, students will be looking for the intensive treatment of a requested skill area that an exercise provides.
3. Students tend to view language classes at this level as awareness-raising opportunities which should enable them to employ their newly acquired expertise autonomously in subsequent real world contexts.

Let us take an example. In the real world, we once taught a student who was given to writing long abstract sociology assignments, which were occasionally obscure and frequently boring. We talked over with him the usefulness of adding illustrations to support his more abstract statements. Exercise 6 (*The use of illustrative examples*) provided a lively class activity soon afterwards, and he entered into the spirit of it enthusiastically. Admittedly, the full benefit of this was not immediately apparent in his own work. He first had to consciously remember to use illustrations, and then to concentrate on using them sparingly and relevantly. But once he did so, his writing felt much more lively. This student's case illustrates how a writing class can service the real world needs of its students.

Once the principle has been accepted of teaching different writing skills by means of exercises which are subsequently related to the total writing activities of the learner, there has to be a decision about what skills to teach in any particular lesson. The earlier sections of this chapter have suggested one way of approaching this question. The next section suggests another, and in chapter 5 we will look still more closely at this area.

3.4 Teacher-determined options

Not all teachers work in contexts where negotiation of course content seems appropriate, although we hope the negotiation exercises suggested in Part 2 will make this a real option in most institutions. Therefore, this section considers criteria for determining the choice of writing skills to work on where this responsibility falls to the teacher alone.

There are obviously conflicting criteria for selecting the exercises that best suit a particular group of learners who need to develop writing skills. It is sensible, provisionally, to choose those that appear to suit your class, but equally it is important to sense when unexpected interests or difficulties make it advisable to change the selection. Some of the principles for selection for the kinds of learners we are talking about include:

— *Selecting according to the focus of exercises.* The exercises in Part 2 are grouped under four major headings: Negotiation, Organization, The sociology of writing, and Techniques. The most obvious strategy is to use these categories as the basis for selection. Within some of the categories are sub-sections, so it may well be that when we are focusing on techniques that we select a sub-section (e.g., Exactness) for a series of related exercises.

— *Selection by linguistic criteria.* You may decide that it would be useful to work with increasingly longer stretches of text – word, sentence, paragraph, whole text – or indeed to reverse the order by starting with the whole text first.

— *Selection for instrumental purposes.* The principle behind instrumental selection is that as a skill is needed or looks as if it will soon be needed, you give the learners a chance to work at an exercise that seeks to focus on the skill. For instance, if you have a group of post-graduate students who are required to write an abstract of an assignment of a thesis, you might select exercise 18 (*How does an abstract differ from a summary?*). You are fulfilling a positive external need.

— *Selection for remedial purposes.* This differs from instrumental selection in that instead of looking forward to possible future needs or even present needs, it is concerned with where learners have already made mistakes through insufficient preparation. You notice, for instance, that learners in your class tend to use 'I' in the wrong circumstances and in the wrong way in their writing. So you prepare to use exercise 14 (*'I' in formal writing*) and introduce it at the first suitable opportunity in your programme. On another occasion, the problem might well be at the macro level and you realize that a proper use of sub-headings would make a substantial difference; you would then select exercise 10 (*Sub-headings*) which has two activities, A and B, that can be used together or separately.

Many sets of exercises are graded according to difficulty, but in exercises of this kind the amount and sophistication of the language used is determined by the knowledge and ability of the class. Indeed, the same exercise may be done at an intermediate or an advanced level. The effect is very similar to what one of us observed in a class of eleven-year-old second language learners in Britain who were asked to write ten sentences about a picture. These varied from the simplest description of the objects in the picture to a careful account of the situation and how it might have occurred. Sometimes selection may be on apparently trivial grounds as, for instance, when the class has been working rather stolidly and you choose an exercise because it contains some particularly lively and interesting activities.

Whatever criteria of selection you choose, it is important to share the reasoning for such decisions with your learners to give them a sense of participation, and of trust in your own carefully considered reasons for what you do, how you do it, and the order you do it in.

3.5   Using the interests and feelings of the class

When the writing process was being discussed, the point was brought out that unless our real interests and feelings are touched on, we will not readily engage in the very considerable struggle that is necessary if we are to get our thoughts on paper.

The first response of many teachers is to say that the main academic work of the student points to an interest area that should be tapped in the English class. This is a particularly attractive strategy when either the learner's interest is genuinely in the main subject of study or when the subject studied is itself instrumental in terms of gaining qualifications or further employment. Under such circumstances, the language course will have obvious face validity.

But there is a second kind of interest, which is interest in other people and the desire to respond to the interest of others in oneself. This is a very strong human characteristic and is not tapped often enough in the English classroom. In one of our classes, for instance, students doing very different subjects were discussing their research with each other as a pre-writing exercise, and it was very interesting to listen to the alert questioning – partly on a personal level – by two or three Middle Eastern Muslim students of a South Korean student who was researching into the early decades of Christianity.

This brings us to the next point: that ideas themselves, political problems, national and cultural differences at almost every level are of interest to most learners. It is important not to stereotype learners and to presume interests that they may not have or that may be less strong than other unexpected interests.

Engagement of feelings is also of considerable importance. When feelings are touched, learners are totally involved in the writing and appear at times to be writing above their expected capability.

The final point we would make is that often it is apparently trivial objects and happenings that are invested with particular personal involvement. Objects such as the contents of our pockets, the pictures or cassettes we own; connections such as our family, friends, and correspondents; and happenings such as how we spent last birthday or the evening after an examination are all personal and very much part of us as people, and as such are interesting to others.

To sum up: we as teachers should start by engaging the interest and personal involvement of the learner by building on learner input, whether it is connected with past experiences, present knowledge, interests, ideas, and personal characteristics, or future hopes, plans or predictions. These things will provide a motivation for writing, as well as the personal stimulus to take the writer through a number of barriers.

3.6 Learner input

In the previous section we have argued strongly for a more person-related input. And in Part 2, the exercises themselves often go further still in this direction, even (in extreme cases) asking learners to treat as input to a writing class such apparently trivial stimuli as the contents of their pockets, their last eating experience and the subject-matter of a week's dreams. This raises a number of questions about the maturity level of the exercise content:

– *How can it be right to apply the sophisticated structuring and organization techniques that are typical of the exercises to such a trivial content?* The purpose of the exercise based on the contents of pockets is to explore a range of ways of expressing degrees of probability. The contents of our pockets, therefore, are like the findings that emerge from a set of laboratory experiments in that some are predictable and some surprising. So we have a direct choice: we can ask the students to bring sets of laboratory results to class or to turn out their pockets. It is precisely the common, human experience of seeing how the contents of the various pockets compare with one's own that makes this exercise so very interesting. Moreover, the data is immediately clear to everyone and the meaning that has to be conveyed in the subsequent writing exercise obvious – the same cannot, unfortunately, be said for laboratory results, as bitter experience in the past has taught us.

There are similar arguments for using last eating experiences as input to an exercise in expressing similarity and difference, or the dreams of groups of students as input to be edited into a report. Ultimately what is crucial is that the writing task should be seen as instrumentally relevant – if the students are satisfied that their writing of authentic laboratory reports benefits from this humanistic indirection, then they will not challenge its maturity level.

And one last point in response to this question: many humanistic teachers would want to argue that the act of revealing such personal things as the contents of our pockets, our last eating experience, and our dreams, in fact binds us together as a group, and is far from trivial.

— *Will my students, will I – come to that – be happy working in this way?* Whilst it is natural to be apprehensive if you have not worked in this way before, you may find that it offers a far more effective solution to the problem of learner motivation than falling back on a routine based around a textbook. The only way of answering this question, anyway, is – try it.

— *In order to mirror the real world of my students, shouldn't specialist academic texts be the input to a writing exercise?* There are several practical problems here: most texts tend to be opaque even to experts – let alone to fellow-students with different backgrounds and interests; few yield humanistic materials of general interest; all take considerable time to read and understand.

However, in a writing class one useful activity is the reformulation of the information extracted from a text. Nevertheless, it may be quicker and simpler to reformulate the raw data on which the text is based. Whilst there is only very limited use for written material as specific input to writing exercises, written texts are often extremely useful in follow-up activities after such exercises. These texts can often be learner-selected and the learner will read them with specific purposes in mind.

And finally, by no means all our writing is based only on previous reading. Talk, discussion, experimentation, survey work, data collection of many other kinds is also important. So it could be argued that the questionnaire element built into the last eating experience exercise and the record keeping and verbal reporting built into the dreams exercise are just as authentic as inputs to writing as texts are.

3.7 Establishing the best learning environment in the classroom

The accepted environment of the classroom is often affected by the 'culture' of the institution and of the country in which it is situated. Students themselves may have particular expectations of how serious work should be done. Furthermore there may be pressures from the authorities, inspectors, religious institutions or families. Individual teachers have a choice between conforming to the pressures on them or quite deliberately choosing to create an atmosphere in the classroom that is more open and learner-centred. This may even be thought of as a political decision: teachers may sometimes choose to be in the van of political change as well as in its wake.

A particular classroom may, of course, have its own atmosphere that does not threaten the ethos of the institution as a whole. For instance, we have observed that, within the schooling system in Britain, the art room in even quite a formal establishment often has a pleasant, relaxed atmosphere. Possibly there is a tape on with quiet music, students are walking around from time to time, and there is a pleasant low hum of conversation. It is very often particularly noticeable how the students trust the teacher and each other. They are prepared to allow fellow-students as well as the teacher to observe their work in progress. Something of this workshop atmosphere needs to be part of the language classroom. At the same time, writing is essentially a private and concentrated activity so there must be islands of quietness and calm. Most importantly, there must be an atmosphere of openness and trust.

Typically, then, one expects a flexible classroom where students are sometimes walking around questioning other individuals, or working in groups, or listening to instructions and feedback as a class. This atmosphere is not necessarily easy to obtain, but it is important to work hard at achieving it to get the best output from the learners.

3.8   Classroom outcomes

In this section, we would like to consider what is likely to happen in a writing class of the kind presupposed by the earlier sections of this chapter. The example we give is a real one. We are going to join one of the three groups of six learners at the point in the lesson where each student had written a sentence and read it aloud. While the other two groups were busily and usefully listening to each other's sentences, and selecting one, the group we are joining has chosen Ahmed's sentence to work with. He had written:

> *Some of the decision-maker, when they feel they have absolute freedom, they don't mind to harm innocent people.*

At this stage, the teacher asked the group to try to improve Ahmed's sentence in a way that he would accept, and that retained its original meaning.

In the hour-long discussion that followed, these were some of the issues raised:
— what percentage was implied by 'some';
— whether 'some decision-makers' was better, or whether 'of the' should be left in and world leaders cited as an example;
— if 'some decision-makers' was preferred, did it not come to the same thing to say simply 'when people have power . . .';

- the significance of 'when they *feel*';
- whether 'freedom' was the right word;
- whether the writer understood the meaning of 'don't mind' and whether the register was appropriate;
- whether 'don't hesitate' was any better;
- whether 'innocent' only meant politically powerless;
- whether or not the writer intended to state that there was a ratio between being politically powerful and being ruthless.

The group were intensely interested in helping Ahmed to express his real meaning as well as possible, and listened to each other's contributions intently, both learning from and helping each other as well as helping Ahmed. However, even with four more suggestions, Ahmed did not feel, although they were more correct linguistically, that they had captured the true meaning of what he wanted to write. Interestingly enough, far from being upset by this, the group respected Ahmed's desire to keep the essential meaning of his statement and were quite happy for him to go away and try to rewrite his sentence taking some of their ideas on board. He was asked to bring his revised version to the next session.

How did Ahmed come to write a sentence that was so important to him that he was not ready to accept any sentences, however grammatically correct, that did not encapsulate his exact meaning? He had been in a class working on exercise 30 (*Proportion, contrast and expressing an exact meaning*). At the beginning of the lesson, his neighbour had completed the questionnaire supplied by the teacher and had added to the starter 'Given absolute freedom to do as you wished, would you . . .' the words '. . . do something to harm people?' The questionnaire had been passed to Ahmed, who had answered the yes/no question for himself and estimated what percentage of people would answer it in the same way. When the teacher asked him to choose just one question on his questionnaire, he had chosen this one to turn into a sentence connecting the question, the typical reaction, and his own opinion. The result was:

> *Some of the decision-maker, when they feel they have absolute freedom, they don't mind to harm innocent people.*

We hope this short section gives you a flavour of what you may expect to be happening in writing classes based on the exercises suggested in Part 2.

3.9 Preparing ahead

When planning to teach a particular lesson we suggest that you have a checklist that you consult briefly before finally deciding on what to teach

and how to teach it. Such a list might well contain some of the following points among others:
- Do the learners need to review, reflect on, or apply the material of the last lesson?
- Have you identified an obvious writing need to focus on?
- Have the learners expressed a need?
- Is it time to consolidate a piece of completed work with a related activity?
- Is there an especially interesting exercise that you and the class feel ready for?

Once the topic has been selected, what further preparation is needed both on the part of the teacher and of the learners?

Learners' preparatory activities tend to be in two directions. The first is the finding and bringing of material that may be used in the writing lesson, e.g., a family photograph or a newspaper article in their first language. The second is preliminary writing to be used in the lesson. Most writing classes are more likely to call for follow-up rather than preparation.

The teacher, on the other hand, after thoroughly researching the possible linguistic outcomes of a particular exercise must be prepared to use that knowledge sparingly and not too overtly. There must be a balance between ignorance on the part of the teacher and being the expert who provides all the ready-made answers. The teacher may, of course, actually have to bring materials to class – even from time to time a piece of writing!

3.10   The follow-up

Some learners are helped by afterwards reflecting on what they have done in class. For instance, following exercise 14 (*'I' in formal writing*) we suggest discussing uses of 'I' other than the tentative use which is the main focus of that particular exercise. We suggest the following stages:
- discussing what has been discovered;
- discussing other uses;
- observing actual usages;
- recording any useful usages in a notebook;
- leaving till last (if one does it at all) looking up particular points in a reference book.

What should be encouraged is the observation of language in use. What should be discouraged is looking up a so-called rule and applying it. There is, of course, the further stage when learners look at their own past work to see strengths and weaknesses in this area and their conscious good use of what has been learned in their next written text.

To illustrate the ways in which we might observe a particular sub-skill in use, we take the notion of disagreeing, which we discussed in chapter 2 and which underlies exercise 13 (*Using counter-arguments*). Because these are essentially awareness raising exercises, by way of a follow-up our learners might well be asked to observe one or more of the following and then share their findings in a subsequent lesson:
— disagreeing in a first-hand spoken English environment outside the classroom (if that is possible);
— disagreeing as observed in a second-hand spoken English environment (e.g., radio programmes or videos);
— disagreeing as observed in less formal writing (e.g., articles in the tabloid press or popular weeklies);
— disagreeing in formal writing (e.g., a journal article).
In the latter exploration we would hope to establish which of the following types of disagreement were more common:
— 'Though Wood has some interesting things to say, there are many inaccuracies in his statement.'
— 'Wood's analysis is wrong.'
— 'We would tend to disagree with Wood's analysis.'
Reference back to what has been discovered in a particular session helps to establish it in the minds of the learners. It is all too easy to treat lessons in isolation.

Finally, we do consider it of considerable importance to help the learner apply what has been learned in the English class to writing elsewhere, both in and outside the institution. One of the best ways of doing the former is to ask learners to look at the element learned (in this case the use of 'I') in the previous two assignments they did in their main subjects, to evaluate how effectively they used it, and to keep this particular element in mind in their next piece of work.

4 Evaluating writing

In the last chapter, we discussed ways of improving writing skills and in this one we discuss whether, how and when to evaluate them. At the same time, we try to broaden traditional notions of evaluation and assessment. We will be considering three positions:
– arguments against evaluating writing;
– some possibilities for evaluating the writing process;
– evaluation of the final product.
Everyone knows that final, formal products often have to be graded/ marked/tested/evaluated/assessed/examined/defended – the list of evaluation measures seems endless. In an EAP context, however, the final, assessable products will typically be subject assignments, theses, research papers, etc., rather than the work produced for the writing class. Assessment of these products will relate primarily to content, but necessarily to form as well. We need to set against this the standard practice in most general (i.e., non-EAP) language classes. Here the teacher typically corrects the written work that is generated, grading it and pointing out surface errors. We think that this sort of evaluation of student writing is not usually appropriate to the outcomes of the exercises in this book. At the same time, we recognize that the contexts in which many teachers work do require language class writing outcomes to be evaluated. We are, therefore, anxious to make suggestions that enable teachers to follow this book's approach to the teaching of writing and at the same time to meet institutional requirements in the field of evaluation, though not so easily of assessment.

A glance at the exercises will indicate the problems involved. They do not set out to measure learner performance against a norm; much of the work is collective and typically focuses on the process of writing. In short, the exercises do not lead to the production of texts suited to direct individual testing or examination. Nevertheless, we hope the three sections that follow will contain some helpful ideas.

4.1 Two arguments against evaluating writing

The first argument against evaluating writing is a general methodological one. Throughout this book we are arguing that the teacher's role is that of an enabler of student self-discovery rather than that of instructor. Furthermore, there is a considerable amount of literature on repair techniques which demonstrates a systematic preference for self-repair or self-correction in native speaker language use. We think that an enabling teacher would want to maximize the possibilities for learner self-correction and that formal evaluation places the kind of emphasis on product that limits learner concentration on process. Ann Chenoweth (1987) argues that:

> Better writers not only have strategies for correcting local problems
> such as word choice, grammar, and punctuation. They also deal with
> overall content and meaning of their writing by adding, deleting, or
> reorganizing larger chunks of discourse as well. Unskilled writers lack
> these global strategies ... teachers of writing should structure their
> classes in ways that will help students expand their repertoire of
> strategies for rewriting compositions.

If she is right, one would want to avoid pre-empting this rewriting by too rapid a move towards evaluation.

The second argument centres on the very real difficulty of evaluating writing. In far too many contexts evaluation is linked to marking down texts exhibiting grammatical inadequacies that have little to do with writing skills. The following quotation from Ann Raimes (1983) enlarges on this point:

> It's no accident that so much attention is paid to grammar in the
> teaching of writing. Grammar is one part of writing that can be
> straightforwardly taught.

It is understandable for teachers to feel a responsibility to point out inaccuracies in their students' English, but we need to remember that accuracy is only one small part of the skill of writing, which includes at least the topic headings under which the exercises in Part 2 are grouped: Organization, Observing cultural constraints, Writing for a purpose, Readership awareness, Expressing complex ideas, Exactness and Writing skills.

The problem of evaluation centres on deciding how to assess learner skill in these, less overt, areas. How, for example, is the teacher to evaluate, in a way that is helpful for the learner, what Shaughnessy (1980) calls 'the failure to stay with a line of thought'? It is because we believe that student collaboration and teacher intervention at the process stage are the best ways of ensuring that 'lines of thought' are developed logically through learner discovery that we are broadly opposed to formal evaluation. In this way, we are working towards an approach which, when successful, renders such evaluation redundant.

Acknowledgement: Much of the research that underlies the position taken in this section of the chapter was the work of Lakshmy Anathakrishnan as part of an unpublished MA dissertation. Readers of her dissertation would recognize our indebtedness to her.

4.2   Evaluating at the process stage

We take it as self-evident that in writing, as well as in speech, self-correction is preferable to peer correction, and peer correction to teacher correction. And because rewriting or self-correction is so important a writing skill, a good teacher will provide the maximum classroom opportunity for it, and indeed will include rewriting ability in any overall evaluation of learners' writing skills.

Thus a teacher will indicate to learners that it is not only the product that is assessable, but that commitment to the process is also expected. What then are the process skills relating to self-correction that a teacher can reasonably evaluate? We think they include:
— Rewriting sentences or paragraphs during the course of their construction in order to enable writers to express their meanings in the ways they would like to. We can call this 'rewriting while writing'. Many of the exercises in Part 2 call for just this skill. When you try them out, you will notice that learners do not always produce improved versions of the original text. We suggest that it would be very proper from time to time to indicate that the rewritten version of a short text will be evaluated alongside and in relation to the original. Those that lend themselves naturally to this technique are exercise 6 (*The use of illustrative examples*), exercise 7 (*Inserting additional material*), exercise 29 (*Towards the language of proportion*), and exercise 32 (*Describing spatial relations*).
— Rewriting with the reader in mind, taking into account his or her previous knowledge, cultural assumptions and linguistic ability. We can call this 'rewriting for the reader'. Exercise 23 (*Taking the reader into account*) provides an obvious way of testing skill in this area since learners can be asked to write on the same topic for several different target readers.
— Rewriting to eliminate distracting features, such as poor punctuation and incorrect spelling. We can call this 'proof-reading', though it involves slightly more than this.

Because the exercises in Part 2 are typically process related and because evaluating writing is so often product related, we thought it might be useful to add a number of proof-reading suggestions to assist learners to self-correct between the apparent end of the process stage and the submission of the product. You may like to use some or all of the boxed sections below for your learners; for this reason, they are written with your learners as their target readership and each carries an ignore-this-at-your-peril health warning: 'Proof-reading is fundamentally . . .' A technique that works well is to ask learners to concentrate on one proof-reading skill per assignment and then for you, the teacher, to evaluate the extent to which the indicated skill has been effectively practised.

WORKSHEET: PROOF-READING I

Proof-reading is fundamentally an activity which shows courtesy to your reader and helps him or her to process the text more easily. Without it, he or she may still be able to make sense of your text, but may be less keen to do so as the process has been made more difficult.

Chunking

One of the most distracting things in looking at a text is to get no help with how to divide it into meaning units. A comma, or sometimes two, in the right place/s can help your reader considerably in the task of phrasing the material intelligibly. In developing this skill, there are two techniques which are useful. The first is to use a reliable reference book on punctuation. The second is to ask a friend to read your writing through and indicate where he or she had to reread sentences to make sense of them.

There are two further strategies that can make for intelligibility. One is dividing long sentences. The longer the sentence, the more unlikely it is that the writer can control linguistically the logical connections between its parts. The other is rearranging the parts of a sentence. The two principles here are to try to keep as near to each other as possible those parts of a sentence that are most closely related, and to put the topic of a sentence as early as possible.

c

WORKSHEET: PROOF-READING 2

Proof-reading is fundamentally an activity which shows courtesy to your reader and helps him or her to process the text more easily. Without it, he or she may still be able to make sense of your text, but may be less keen to do so as the process has been made more difficult.

Spelling

Incorrect spelling (including typing or word processing errors) distract the reader rather than impede comprehension. Two useful techniques are:
– identifying words of whose spellings you are uncertain;
– getting a colleague to look out for spelling errors.
This is also an area in which keeping a language file is particularly useful. The language file will alert you to past errors and will contain a brief list of your most commonly misspelt words.

Where you are doubtful about a spelling, it is best to be consistent. For example, if 'paralyse' apears four times in a text, it is better not to write 'paralize ... paralyse ... paralize ... paralyse' in the hope that two of the spellings are right! In genuinely difficult cases of this sort, *Hart's Rules for Compositors and Readers* is particularly useful.

On the whole, it is better to keep to either British or American spelling and to be consistent about that too. However, in some fields the influence of the United States is so strong that British writers in those fields are beginning to adopt American spellings. For instance, in computing literature 'programme' is often spelt 'program'. In such cases you may, of course, do the same.

WORKSHEET: PROOF-READING 3

Proof-reading is fundamentally an activity which shows courtesy to your reader and helps him or her to process the text more easily. Without it, he or she may still be able to make sense of your text, but may be less keen to do so as the process has been made more difficult.

Punctuation

Being consistent in the way you use punctuation is very important. This is especially true of capitals (which should be used sparingly) and underlining (when it is used as an alternative to inverted commas for the titles of books, journals, and articles). In the same way it is important to be consistent in using commas after sentence modifiers such as 'however' when they are initial, but on each side when they are in other positions.

The use of semi-colons is fairly sophisticated and you should typically choose between commas and full stops, the latter being often underused. The alternative of adding a connecting word and keeping the comma will sometimes be best. The use of hyphens in compounds, especially made up adjectives used attributively, is often inconsistent in English. Many native speakers have never been taught the recognized ways of breaking up long words that do not fit into the space at the end of a line – have you?

You can check those things of which you are uncertain in a book such as *Hart's Rules for Compositors and Readers*.

WORKSHEET: PROOF-READING 4

Proof-reading is fundamentally an activity which shows courtesy to your reader and helps him or her to process the text more easily. Without it, he or she may still be able to make sense of your text, but may be less keen to do so as the process has been made more difficult.

Stylistic inelegance

The English hate rhyme, near rhyme and verbal repetition in prose writing. The following two examples of learner writing show this: 'Muslims pray five times a day'; 'The effect that substances like weedkillers have when used in conjunction with substances like fertilizers is that too many substances are going into the water supplies and these substances...'

A second common stylistic fault is to be too uniform, particularly in sentence length and type. Where there are no more than a series of very short simple sentences in a piece of writing, for instance, it is easy for the reader to dismiss the thought as simplistic and to find difficulty in seeing where the emphasis of a paragraph should be.

A third stylistic fault is lack of proper division into paragraphs, which is, of course, compounded when there is also a lack of sub-headings.

WORKSHEET: PROOF-READING 5

Proof-reading is fundamentally an activity which shows courtesy to your reader and helps him or her to process the text more easily. Without it, he or she may still be able to make sense of your text, but may be less keen to do so as the process has been made more difficult.

Grammatical awkwardness

Most learners have faults which they have learned to eliminate consciously but which nevertheless creep back into their work when they are writing fast. Whether your problems are with articles, verb endings, the use of properly collocated negatives (i.e., 'that is unimportant at all' when 'that is not at all important' is intended), you will often be able to spot most of these mistakes (with or without the help of a colleague) simply by rereading carefully. It is worth taking the time to be accurate in these problem areas since your work will be much more acceptable if you do.

Some of the exercises in Part 2, for example, exercise 38 (*Cohesion*), exercise 42 (*Punctuation*), exercise 44 (*Synthesis*), focus on skills referred to in the five boxed sections above, so that you could, if you wished, use an exercise as a lead-in to focusing on a proof-reading skill.

We hope you will agree that proof-reading is both important and trivial. It is important because a piece of writing that has not been proof-read will irritate readers, impede rapid understanding, and cause readers to think that the writer is less intelligent and educated than may be the case. It is trivial because it is only the surface weaknesses that are usually dealt with in proof-reading and it does not, therefore, deal with those aspects of the text that cause incomprehension or misunderstanding. Nevertheless, proof-reading is important and we think that this way of focusing on, and even evaluating commitment to, accuracy and intelligibility at the post-process, pre-product stage will help learners to become autonomous and effective proof-readers. No one wants their students to follow in the footsteps of a Ph.D. student of high calibre in our faculty who recently submitted an original and thoughtful thesis, and found himself having to resubmit simply because the typographical errors were so numerous. Had the quality of his work been in serious doubt, the poor proof-reading would not have helped his case.

4.3   Evaluation of the product

The position we have been arguing for so far is that learner self-evaluation is ultimately more important than teacher evaluation of learner writing. Indeed, assessment will reflect to some extent the less instructional and more enabling role for the teacher assumed in the exercises. Follow-up suggestions for particular exercises in Part 2 are typically aimed at promoting either learner self-evaluation or the conscious carry-over by learners of skills acquired in the writing session to contexts outside the language classroom.

Other activities that promote self-monitoring and self-evaluation during subsequent writing and which can occur naturally as a follow-up to many of the exercises include:
- reflection on the kind of language practised;
- investigation of the focus of the lesson in other materials (e.g., looking at the use of illustrations or the function of abstracts in books or articles after the exercises on those themes);
- reassessment of writing that has already been completed outside the language class by the learner him- or herself;
- paying attention in the next piece of writing completed outside the language classroom to the focus of the previous exercise.
It may often be useful to ask the subject teacher to look out for evidence

that the language skills recently taught are surfacing in learners' writing. In some institutions the English teacher and the subject teacher are also able to co-operate in assessing the needs of the students and in evaluating some of the written products that are generated during the course of the year.

A genuine problem faced by some teachers is an overemphasis within the educational system itself on grading. This can result in the stifling of experimentation and relaxed practice. It is important to work towards an atmosphere where activities are valued whether they lend themselves to being red-pencilled and graded by the teacher or not. Process activities (except where they are particularly product-like) are better not graded.

However, if formal evaluation is required of a language teacher working with this book, special care will be necessary in choosing a suitable exercise. Very often the point of an exercise is to practise a process skill – formal evaluation of a product will obviously be out of place here. But when an exercise does lead to a clear product, for example, exercise 4 (*Linking paragraphs*), then clearly formal teacher evaluation is perfectly possible. And in fact, it may be particularly helpful for learners to be given some indication of how effective their writing is seen to be after it has gone through three or four versions, as in this particular exercise. Even then it will be easier to evaluate it in general terms than to award a grade or a mark.

A word of warning: in the case of exercise 4 (*Linking paragraphs*), the evaluation will be of a piece of writing produced by four learners working collaboratively. This obviously provides opportunities for encouraging all to perform at the limit of their ability. At the same time, it may require a degree of careful handling where a highly competitive learner feels that only his or her sole efforts should be assessed. Approximately one in four of the exercises lead to product-like individual writing suitable for teacher evaluation. They include exercise 10 (*Sub-headings A*), exercise 11 (*Using sources*), exercise 16 (*Question or statement?*), and exercise 26 (*Relating one's own findings to primary texts*).

4.4 Summary

It must be the case that only the learners can truly judge how their written English is improving and the extent to which they have their teachers to thank for this increased awareness.

We tend to take the view that formal evaluation inhibits self-correction at the vital process stage because it is product/accuracy-driven rather than 'line of thought' related. Nevertheless, in this chapter, we have tried to suggest a range of techniques for putting the kind of evaluative measures typically available to teachers into the hands of learners too.

We hope that this shared methodology will promote effective, autonomous, learner writing.

We have also suggested a set of exercises where formal product evaluation can be viewed as positive, and consistent with the spirit of our approach. You may think it appropriate to use one exercise in three, say, as a way of evaluating learner writing. In this way, both teachers and learners may see how the ideas underlying this approach to teaching writing can serve the same curriculum purposes as more traditional approaches.

5 Getting the best out of this book in the classroom

In chapter 3 we looked at the general practice of teaching writing, based on the principles which lie behind the exercises in this book. In this chapter we look at specific points connected with using this book in the classroom.

5.1 How this book works

There are 44 exercises in Part 2, all of which are self-contained, and so can be thought of as independent units. We have grouped them under various headings ourselves, and a number of other suggestions for grouping them are made in section 5.2 (Choosing an exercise). We expect that most teachers will choose one of our suggested methods of general grouping and at the same time work out a particular sequence of exercises to suit their classes.

The exercises are set out in four sub-sections:

Focus – where we try to define the writing area dealt with and suggest reasons for viewing it as important.

Class organization – where we suggest ways of grouping the class for the exercise, and give an indication of time and materials required.

The exercise – where we provide a numbered series of stages that the learners are expected to follow. These are written up in a way that combines instruction (i.e., what to do) with description (i.e., what might be expected to happen). We hope that you will think this through before your lesson, and try to imagine how it will work in practice, making whatever changes or amendments are appropriate for your class. Frequently you will find that more than one instruction is grouped under each numbered stage. This is because we are trying to discourage the too slavish following of a seven or eight step lesson.

Comments – where we suggest ways of reinforcing what has been practised with futher work and helping learners to reflect on the activity they have been engaged in by thinking about its wider applicability, and especially its relevance to future academic writing tasks of various kinds.

5.2   Choosing an exercise

We have four specific points to make about choosing exercises:
- Remember to consider both the *focus* and the *activity* involved before choosing an exercise to work with. For instance, it would be worth looking carefully at exercises 27, 28 and 29 which deal with comparison, correspondence, and proportion to see which of these not dissimilar focuses is most helpful. It would also be worth looking equally carefully at the activities involved in each of the three exercises. Exercise 28 (*Correspondence and non-correspondence*), which is to do with struggling to make sense of a newspaper article written in a language unknown to the reader, is the more unusual. Therefore you might not want to use it at an early stage of the course, preferring either to defer or adapt it. (Although where such an activity succeeds, it provides a really memorable part of the programme.)
- The fact that we have suggested that the exercises could be grouped according to criteria such as text length or difficulty does not mean that such groupings need to be rigidly adhered to. For instance, it might be useful to alternate exercises that deal with long stretches of text and those that deal with sentences, rather than first deal with all of one kind and then all of another. So it might well be helpful to juxtapose exercise 30 (*Proportion, contrast and expressing an exact meaning*) where only a sentence is written with exercise 6 (*The use of illustrative examples*) where a longer passage is attempted.
- When you select exercises according to your students' needs and interests, you will probably be keeping automatically to some of the other criteria, such as level of difficulty, instrumental usefulness or remedial need.
- It is important to identify at the beginning of the programme those points which it is essential to cover; equally, one needs to be genuinely flexible and attentive to particular needs and wishes as they arise.

5.3   Preparing for the lesson

After the selection of an exercise , the next stage is to work through a checklist of pre-class preparation activities such as the following:
1. *What, if any, preliminary work or observation do the learners need to do? Do they need to bring any materials to class?* For example, in exercise 7 (*Inserting additional material*) it will be necessary for students to bring a previously completed assignment to class, or in exercise 19 (*The written evaluation*) the students are required to bring a written homework to class.
2. *What motivating strategies will ensure that learners are fully engaged*

in the lesson? Selecting exercises whose activities are, or can be made, interesting to a particular group of students is important. Part of the reason for choosing exercise 19 (*The written evaluation*) in preference to one of the other exercises that focuses on report-type writing may well be that, in your estimation, discussion by each pair of the way they would get home quickly in an emergency would be intrinsically interesting. Equally important is instrumental motivation and this particular exercise could be made attractive to the learners by talking through the importance of evaluation in academic writing, spiced (where possible) with anecdotes or illustrations.

3. *Is a particular classroom lay-out required?* If you are setting up the room for exercise 12 (*Entering caveats*), it might well be sensible to get your class sitting in groups of three at the beginning of the session rather than at the point we suggest, even though they will start by working individually.

4. *What materials are required for the lesson? What contingency materials will be needed if the learners fail to bring anything they were asked to?* For example, exercise 31 (*Revealing attitudes*) requires two types of materials – news items and stationery items. The absence of either would make the lesson an impossibility.

5. *What strategies are required for dealing with slower or faster groups?* In exercise 6 (*The use of illustrative examples*), groups have to prepare a written passage together and this is passed on to the next group for processing when ready. Inevitably students work at different speeds. However, this can be used to make slower groups work faster. One way to assist them to do this is for you to sit with such a group and help them in formulating ideas. Faster groups in the meanwhile can use extra time for discussion. In this particular exercise a fast group can even select a second scribe to try another passage.

6. *How long will each section of the lesson take? Are there sections that can be speeded up in the event of time difficulties?* Exercise 31 (*Revealing attitudes*) can be run as one or two sessions. You can even leave this decision till you are actually working with the class and are better able to judge how fast they are able to work together.

7. *What role will the teacher have at each stage?* The decision not to interfere at certain crucial stages is important but particularly difficult to implement as learners are struggling to find the language with which to express an idea. In exercise 30 (*Proportion, contrast and expressing an exact meaning*), for example, you may well decide to join a group, but you will have to impose a rule of total silence on yourself if you do.

8. *Precisely how will each instruction be given?* Thinking hard before the class about framing instructions so that they provide really clear and unambiguous guidelines for the learners is particularly important.

Take the case of exercise 4 (*Linking paragraphs*): this is one of the most rewarding exercises in the classroom but will be a disaster if the instructions are not given clearly.

5.4   Class structure and strategies

Pre-class preparation obviously goes beyond the practical points listed in the previous section. It also involves considering other, less mechanical aspects of classroom dynamics and teacher stance. In this section and the following one, we consider some of these. It may be helpful to choose a fairly simple activity like exercise 17 (*Writing a forecast*), and try it with a class, before coming back to the seven points listed below.

1. *If an atmosphere of trust is to be engendered in the classroom, you will have to work towards an open classroom.* Several examples require the learners to express their true ambitions, opinions, or feelings in an atmosphere of trust. Exercise 37 (*Accounting for facts*) is a typical exercise of this kind.

2. *One of the ways of working towards openness is for the teacher to participate equally in those activities that require frankness. Thus learners should not be expected to reveal the contents of their pockets or talk about their last eating experience unless the teacher joins in too.* In exercise 18 (*How does an abstract differ from a summary?*), the teacher also has to do the homework and bring it to class for evaluation.

   Openness is also more easily achieved where learners work in small groups or in pairs, thus diminishing the 'on trial' atmosphere that is sometimes present in the classroom.

3. *As a teacher, you have to be very alert to how the lesson is going and be adaptable in the way you monitor and assist with its progress.* When you try exercise 20 (*Impersonal writing and probability*), you may conceivably find that some of your learners do not have the six required objects in their possession. In that case you may decide that it is sensible for learners to write down on small bits of card what they had in their pockets/handbags yesterday or the day before yesterday.

4. *As a teacher, you may be torn between two opposite built-in feelings. On the one hand you may believe that only perfect work should be displayed on the walls. On the other hand, you may have the conviction that it is very useful to display work that you intend to build on with the students even though such work is of itself necessarily imperfect.* Exercise 12 (*Entering caveats*) is a typical example where the cards with sentences stating views with due caution have to be displayed so that groups can decide whether they are in the right order. At the end of the class when students are

actually recording ways of expressing caveats, the teacher might intervene to change the wording here and there or add further examples as a result of discussion.

5. *Make sure that students get used to working with the graphs and the other forms in which information is sometimes presented.* In exercise 5 (*Generalization*), the results of the learners' class surveys are to be represented as graphs, Venn diagrams, histograms, etc., which are then interpreted in continuous prose. Rather than give formal work on these, assist each group to use a suitable one.

6. *The exercises encourage as much full and free discussion as is possible in your institutional set-up. They also require the teacher to provide learners with opportunities for reading the work of their colleagues. This is because mixing the four skills is an important aspect of the exercises. This may involve changing grouping along the way to provide for maximum discussion, and very often requires a flexible classroom around which learners can move when appropriate.* In exercise 8 (*Ordering material*), the original reading was the letters received at home. In class, the grouping is based on the numbers of letters groups of learners have received. This involves initial movement round the room. Discussion of the types of letters and making the essay plan follows. This is a rare chance for working with others at an important stage of planning. The same is true of the next phase when two groups join together. The classroom has to be flexible enough for any two groups who happen to finish at the same time to join each other.

7. *Follow-up work, which may include reflection on what has been done, sharing of both knowledge and problems, and noting down items of grammar and vocabulary, is clearly of great importance.* At the end of exercise 39 (*Collocation in the noun phrase*), it is worth discussing at some length the conventional nature of many English collocations and the usefulness of learning the combination as a single phrase and noting it down as such.

5.5 Teacher role

The two preceding sections have obvious implications for the role of the teacher in facilitating these writing exercises. Clearly the degree of pre-class preparation required is very great, whilst the actual involvement in the lesson once under way will often be relatively small and largely involve servicing learner needs. This may well be a different role for the teacher than that assumed by some coursebooks.

Thus the teacher's conventional role as an instructor diminishes as the learners are encouraged to work together and make discoveries for themselves. The provision of a more flexible classroom follows naturally from accepting that learners group and re-group as they move through a series of tasks. This calls for flexible organization and careful judgements as to when each phase of an exercise has been completed.

If the traditional classroom was one in which the encounter between teacher and learner was an encounter of unequals, these exercises offer the possibility of the teacher working as an equal within a group which learners have formed. If this has never happened in your classroom before, it is not going to happen suddenly tomorrow. And it would be undesirable to try and make the change too quickly because the result would certainly be a group containing but still dominated by the teacher. How then to achieve this greater equality in the classroom?

Broadly one can see a progression from the teacher-dominated class where the teacher both specifies the tasks and leads the class through them to one where the teacher takes no active part in working through the specified tasks. The next stage is the move from whole-class teaching to group work, the teacher, however, still maintaining a role as consultant to any group who requires his or her expertise. Finally, the teacher can become an equal member of a learner group. This can be demonstrated in diagram form:

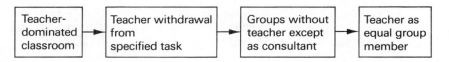

To get from one side of the diagram to the other may take a teacher many months of unlearning established methods and learning new ones. And it may take each new class you meet several weeks to understand and accept this more equal kind of teacher.

Becoming an equal member of the learner group implies a whole range of behaviours including:
- the ability to withdraw and allow the learners to discover for themselves;
- accepting that the less the teacher does, the more the learner does and, specifically, that natural discussion is not possible when dominated by the teacher;
- encouraging self- and peer-correction, and systematically avoiding teacher correction;
- learning to be a convenient, and sometimes fallible, information source, a time-keeper, and a referee in cases of dispute, without becoming at the same time an authority figure;
- actively seeking and respecting the opinions of learners;
- not asking learners to do things you are not prepared to do yourself;

– working within a learner group whilst at the same time giving the necessary instructions to the whole class;
– providing good reasons to the class for those occasions when you are not working with them as an equal.

Some humanistic methodologies have likened the role of the teacher to that of the counsellor, supposing that the best teacher is a non-judgemental listener whose presence encourages the members of the group to bring to the surface what is hidden within them. If you incline towards this role rather than that of the instructor or pedagogue, it is likely to make the writing exercises in Part 2 work properly, and to free teachers who are anxious about their own ability to provide perfect models from the anxiety of having to do so – thus taking away what for some teachers is their major insecurity.

5.6 Group work

Almost all the exercises involve pair or group work. There are a number of reasons for this:
– It encourages collaborative writing.
– It enables you to work with various class sizes.
– It enables more students to talk in English more of the time.
– It enables groups to compare their work with that of other groups.
– It means that the individual learner is less exposed, especially in those exercises where the group take responsibility for a written outcome.
– It allows the teacher's role to be redefined.

Although this is not a book about working in groups, there are a number of aspects of group work that we would like to comment on briefly. They include attitudes to group work, setting up groups, and the group at work.

Attitudes to group work

For those of us who have become so familiar with group work as to take it as natural, it is all too easy to forget that working in small groups is the exception rather than the rule in most educational institutions world-wide. Therefore one needs to think carefully about learner expectations: do our learners come from a culture where small group work has been established for twenty years, for ten years, or where it happens only in English language classes?

If our learners are not used to working in small groups, they may well think that it is not a mode that enables learning and doubt the value of peer contact altogether. And in a society where authority figures (e.g., politicians, the military, mothers, fathers, the church) are strongly respected, there may also be expectations about the role of the teacher that our learner-centred approach falls foul of. We therefore need to take special care to justify small group work to our learners.

Setting up groups

Although almost all the exercises in this book require group or pair work, we rarely make suggestions as to how a group or a pairing might be set up. In exercise 11 (*Using sources*), we do say, 'Ask students to pair themselves with a fellow student who is not a close friend but to whom they feel they can talk openly', but this sort of suggestion is comparatively rare in the exercises as a whole. How then should groups be set up?

Often one is happy for learners to group themselves, although one may ask them to work with a variety of fellow students, or in a mixed language class not to work with speakers of the same mother tongue.

But many teachers intuitively feel it their responsibility to group students, and so proceed to divide classes themselves. This seems to us difficult to justify since a group is not really formed simply by telling x, y and z to work together. And in any other context, the client would rebel: 'You three go to that counter', in the bank, or, 'You, you and you to this checkout', in the supermarket! If we really want learners to learn from each other, such a directive way of grouping them seems to suggest that the teacher has not absorbed the principles of humanistic teaching, and still wants to retain an authority that conflicts with the decision to have the class work in small groups.

An alternative that works well is to find ways of grouping learners according to some common property they share but did not know about. A good example where one wants to divide a class into three groups as is required for exercise 1 (*Summarizing collective opinions*), is to form groups on the following basis:

Group 1 – students whose birthdays fall earlier in the year than those of their parents.
Group 2 – students whose birthdays fall later in the year than those of their parents.
Group 3 – students whose birthdays fall between those of their parents.

Or where several small groups are required, ask students to form groups with colleagues who had the same or similar childhood career ambitions: nurses, teachers, train-drivers, dictators, etc. Thus each group will have something interesting and perhaps worth thinking about for a moment. Other criteria for group formation include similar experiences, dissimilar physical, personality or interest traits.

Once a class gets accustomed to grouping for reasons that reveal the similarities and differences between people, this becomes an accepted part of classroom behaviour and encourages trust, a corporate sense of well-being, mutual interest and real closeness between learners.

The group at work

There are some practical things that are worth keeping in mind:

1. Most people can work happily together but there can be a problem of group dynamics and group leadership. Just as juries find ways of choosing foremen or women, so groups very often cope with leadership choice. Where this is not working, it may help to intervene tactfully. This is very important if the same people are always getting chosen as group leaders or as scribes.

    There may even be occasions on which you may wish to consider more overt ways of drawing attention to the skills necessary for small group work. A technique we have used to good effect in language classes is to ask groups to complete a modified version of the Osgood Semantic Scale handout suggested for exercise 23 (*Taking the reader into account*), to which we usually add opposites like *black/white*, *brainy/brawny*, *old/young*. Each group completes a handout for their country's first astronaut, or their own ideal spouse. Once the handout is complete, we reveal that the real purpose of the exercise was to practise contributing appropriately to a group decision, and we ask each member of the group to assess the quality of and reasons for his or her contribution. Once groups have discovered the purpose of the exercise, several of them have decided without prompting to repeat the exercise in a more careful way.

2. Full participation in group work is important, but despite what was said immediately above, it is worth noting that often quiet group members are actually fully involved.

3. It is particularly important to work towards a really relaxed atmosphere in the groups. Language learning is as difficult if the learners are tense as it is if they are unmotivated. Some people think that being very explicit about more distant goals at every point makes for a relaxed class; but we have found that simply enjoying the activities together (once the learners have come to trust the facilitator of those activities) decreases the tension in the class, especially if it is known that there will be a full discussion afterwards.

5.7   Teaching a particular exercise

In this section we try to describe from both learner and teacher perspectives how one of the exercises in Part 2 actually works out in the classroom. We have chosen exercise 4 (*Linking paragraphs*) to demonstrate this. The exercise requires a minimum of twelve students in the class, and we once tried it (with a measure of success – and chaos) with a class of 120 Italian teachers! You may like to read exercise 4 now, before returning to this section.

The following description has been set out as an internal dialogue from both a teacher's and a student's point of view.

Student: We've been asked to form groups of four, and the teacher has written several different topics on the blackboard and asked each group to choose one. Our group has chosen 'South Africa today'.

Teacher: I was careful to make sure that each group chose a different topic – I did this by rubbing out each topic as it was chosen by a group.

Student: Each member of the class has now been given a small square of white card and asked to write a brief paragraph about our chosen topic on it.

Teacher: I'm watching now to make sure that there's absolute silence and that each individual writes without consulting neighbours.

Student: Now that we've finished writing, we've been asked to read each of the paragraphs written by the people in our group. Our group is reading silently and passing the cards round from person to person.

Teacher: While they were reading, I put four pieces of circular grey card on each table.

Student: Impossible! – now we've been asked to decide on a logical order for our four paragraphs and to write linking passages on the four pieces of grey card.

Teacher: I was careful to explain that they needed to put one piece of circular grey card in front of each piece of square white card, and that the links could be anything from single words like 'whereas' to quite long sentences. I also insisted that no rewriting of the original paragraphs was allowed.

Student: We've decided on an order and written the links. So now we've called the teacher over to be told what to do next. The teacher has come over, given us enough Blu-tack to stick our writing up on the wall and told us that once our writing is up on the wall, we should find another group's writing, read it carefully, decide on the most important link on their grey cards, and cross it out.

Teacher: It's better to explain what to do next to each group individually. This allows me to make sure that they've got circle–square–circle–square–circle–square–circle–square completed.

It's also important to explain that a group may read as many other groups' pieces of writing and cross out one grey link on each one as they can until one of their own links is crossed out.

Student: Another group has crossed out one of our links and so we have to take our writing off the wall, go back to our table, and decide on a different way of linking our paragraphs.

Teacher: It's important to make sure that each group which has had one of their links crossed out understands that they can't use the same idea again – it's not the words only that they must change, but the idea too. I explained to each group that they might do better to reorganize the order of all four of their paragraphs, and that the only writing they were allowed to do was to replace the link that had been crossed out.

Student: Now that we've found a new way of linking our paragraphs and attached our writing to the wall again, we're setting off once more to cross out another group's best link.

Teacher: There was a lot of activity and some noise in the classroom. I stopped the exercise when most groups had repaired their own writing three times.

Student: The teacher has asked each group to decide on the best way of linking together paragraphs that we tried and to make a nice copy of our four paragraph essay to display on the wall.

Teacher: In this final phase the groups are discovering how important a part the linking between paragraphs plays in the structure of an essay, whether the paragraphs have similar or contrasting contents. The extent to which an essay can be made out of them will depend to a considerable extent on the way they are linked.

We hope that this description will interest general language teachers, as well as EAP specialists, in our exercises. A classroom produced example of what this exercise led to for one group of learners can be found in Part 2 on p. 82. This provides no more than an indication of the kind of outcome to be expected. The attraction of this kind of work is that the outcome is shaped by and is suited to the variety of groups who are capable of working in this way.

PART 2 THE EXERCISES

Introduction

This is the more substantial part of the book and contains 44 writing exercises based on the principles discussed in Part 1, but before moving on to them, we discuss the principles underlying the grouping or sequencing of the exercises.

In the introduction to Part 1, we wrote: '...it is those processes of writing that come as second nature to the expert which are difficult for the learner'. They certainly include:
- knowing what to write about;
- organizing the information to be conveyed;
- deciding on the relative prominence to be given to any particular point;
- incorporating what one learns from listening and reading;
- expressing complex ideas appropriately;
- understanding and respecting cultural constraints;
- understanding and taking account of genres;
- knowing, and then persuading, one's readers;
- rewriting (including expressing meaning exactly and writing accurately).

If one accepts that classroom time should be spent on what is difficult or problematical for the learner, then these elements of the writing process are what one should focus on. In organizing the exercises, we have been anxious to try to relate them to these perceived difficulties in the writing process. They are therefore grouped under four major headings which subsume these perceived difficulties, and are central to effective academic writing:

NEGOTIATON
This section contains exercises to use at the beginning of a writing course when establishing a negotiated syllabus.

ORGANIZATION
This section includes exercises which practise knowing what to write about, organizing the information to be conveyed, deciding on the relative prominence to be given to particular points, and incorporating what one learns from listening and reading.

THE SOCIOLOGY OF WRITING

This is divided into three sub-groups: *Observing cultural constraints*, including understanding and respecting cultural constraints; *Writing for a purpose*, including developing an understanding of and taking account of genres; and *Readership awareness*, which concentrates on assessing, and then persuading, one's readers.

TECHNIQUES

This final section also contains three sub-groups: *Expressing complex ideas*, *Exactness* and *Writing skills*, which focus on rewriting (including expressing meaning exactly and writing accurately).

It should be stressed that these are practice exercises to raise the consciousness of the student in a wide range of areas important in academic writing. The purpose of each exercise is, therefore, to help students to become aware of what is required in academic writing (the desired product) by working on the process by which it is arrived at. At the same time, it is obviously not safe to assume that having worked through an exercise students will be 100 per cent proficient in the area practised. Inevitably this approach involves a great deal of discussion as the thinking process is verbalized and shared in class, so you may sometimes find that the amount of talking that gets done is as great as the amount of writing. This will be particularly true in those classes where the wider relevance and applicability of what has been learnt is also discussed.

All 44 exercises are listed in the contents. You may like to try the first exercise listed in each group or sub-group to begin with, as it should be reasonably straightforward to organize and is likely to appeal to a wide range of learners. (See exercises 1, 4, 11, 17, 23, 26, 30 and 36.) Subsequent exercises are listed alphabetically.

Negotiation

1   Summarizing collective opinions

FOCUS

The term *summarizing* can be used to refer to two rather different processes. It may mean making a summary of a single lengthy text, or it may mean collecting lots of disparate material into a more coherent whole that reflects the extent to which particular views predominate. This exercise is about making a coherent whole out of lots of disparate pieces of information. Exercise 18 (*How does an abstract differ from a summary?*) gives practice in the reduction of a single lengthy text.

The exercise also has the secondary aim of uncovering the perceived needs and problems of a writing class. It therefore makes a useful first lesson on a writing course where a degree of syllabus negotiation is appropriate (see Part 1, p. 40).

CLASS ORGANIZATION

Grouping: In the first phase students work as individuals, later the class
   divides into three groups.
Time: 60 minutes.
Materials: Three sheets of different coloured card.

THE EXERCISE

1. Give each student three small pieces of different coloured card. On the first piece of card (colour A), the student names the *type* of writing he or she most often needs to do (e.g., note-taking, essay writing, summarizing); on the second piece of card (colour B), the most problematic writing *skill* (eg., spelling, paragraphing); and on the final piece (colour C), the most problematic *function* (e.g., using sources, illustrating arguments, organizing ideas).
2. All the colour A cards should be attached to one wall, all the colour B to another, and all the colour C to a third.
3. Divide the class into three groups which will each work on a different area (i.e., type of writing, writing skill or writing function). Each group should make a written summary of the writing needs of the class as evidenced on their wall.
4. End the session with a discussion focusing on what areas need to be

worked on and the order in which these will be addressed. Since most EAP courses are support or service courses at which attendance is voluntary, working out a timetable for subsequent sessions enables students to decide which classes they need to attend.

COMMENTS

One reason for starting an EAP writing course with an exercise on summarizing is that students typically put it at the top of their needs list as studying always involves collating information from a wide range of sources (e.g., books, articles). This exercise points to several good study techniques – the recording of important information on (index) cards, the sequencing of this information, the subsequent amalgamation of it into a coherent text, and its further use for a larger purpose. These are all matters that may be raised in the post-exercise discussion, as are the differences between the particular summary types and experiences which students have encountered in their specialist academic fields.

Acknowledgement: This exercise was thought out with our colleague Julian Edge.

2   Profiling learner ability and need

FOCUS

This exercise focuses on ways of describing degrees of similarity. Although comparable in many ways to exercise 27 (*Comparison – similarity and difference*) it is also a class-wide comparison, and is structured so as to emphasize, first, ways of expressing the generality of one's experience, and, subsequently, ways of expressing its particularity.

Because its subject-matter is learner ability and need, it is particularly suitable as an introductory unit to a writing course based on the exercises in this book. In addition, the categories on the handout that accompanies the exercise relate closely to the topics of other exercises, so it is a simple matter to select exercises in those areas where the students indicate needs.

CLASS ORGANIZATION

Grouping: Students work as individuals.
Time: Up to 60 minutes.
Materials: Two handouts for each learner (see p. 78).

THE EXERCISE

1. Distribute two handouts to each member of the class, which they should complete. Encourage students to ask about headings whose

WORKSHEET: PROFILING LEARNER ABILITY AND NEED

Name

CHECKLIST 1: YOUR LANGUAGE NEEDS

You may need to improve your English for one of two reasons: either you recognize that you need to improve in a particular area, or there is a certain writing skill that you need to acquire. Please tick any of the boxes below that describe an area in which you need to improve.

Organizing ideas ☐

Understanding English writing customs ☐

Particular types of writing ☐

Taking the reader into account ☐

Expressing complex ideas ☐

Accurate writing ☐

Writing skills ☐

CHECKLIST 2: YOUR LANGUAGE ABILITIES

You will already be good at many kinds of writing. Please assess your ability in each of the following areas by ticking the appropriate box.

Linking paragraphs

GOOD	AVERAGE	POOR

Illustrating arguments

GOOD	AVERAGE	POOR

Making generalizations

GOOD	AVERAGE	POOR

Using sources

GOOD	AVERAGE	POOR

Questioning set ideas

GOOD	AVERAGE	POOR

Forecasting

GOOD	AVERAGE	POOR

Summarizing

GOOD	AVERAGE	POOR

Reporting

GOOD	AVERAGE	POOR

Being aware of the reader

GOOD	AVERAGE	POOR

Selecting ideas for readers

GOOD	AVERAGE	POOR

Relating own ideas to existing knowledge

GOOD	AVERAGE	POOR

Comparing

GOOD	AVERAGE	POOR

Being exact

GOOD	AVERAGE	POOR

Verb tenses

GOOD	AVERAGE	POOR

Prepositions

GOOD	AVERAGE	POOR

Punctuation

GOOD	AVERAGE	POOR

Long sentences

GOOD	AVERAGE	POOR

meanings they are unsure of. Each student sticks one copy of their completed handout to the wall.

2. Ask each student to write three or four paragraphs comparing their profiles with those on the wall. This will mean that students are constantly gathering data from the wall, writing, gathering more data, writing again, etc. The first paragraph each student writes should focus on *needs*, and particularly on those general needs of the class that are shared by the writer. Subsequent paragraphs should focus on the writer's *abilities*, and the extent to which they are comparable to those of the class as a whole and/or any other individual in the class.

COMMENTS

There are two possible follow-up exercises:

1. Ask students to underline the comparing expressions in their writing and pin the passage to the wall. Members of the class put together a vocabulary guide based on the underlined language.
2. Pin the finished writing to the wall and ask the students to study it carefully and draw up a syllabus for the next few lessons.
3. It is worth pointing out to students that the categories in Checklist 1 of the handout match those in Checklist 2 — a fact not usually apparent to students as they work on the exercise. Thus *Organizing ideas* matches *Linking paragraphs*, *Illustrating arguments* and *Making generalizations*, *Understanding English writing customs* matches *Using sources* and *Questioning set ideas*, and so on. Very often students will have ticked both a need and an ability in the same area. This may lead to a discussion of the extent to which the way information is sought influences its nature and the implications of this for their own research.
4. As an out of class activity it is often a good idea to encourage students to:
   - spend a few minutes each day with an academic textbook looking for comparing expressions;
   - review the last piece of work submitted to their subject department and see to what extent comparison was well handled;
   - think carefully about how they will draw comparisons in their current main subject assignment.

3 Making an offer

FOCUS

The aim of this exercise is to help students to organize ideas and information in a concise letter of a certain type (the offer or contract). Its secondary function is to establish the basis of an understanding between class and tutor at the start of a course.

Part 2   The exercises

CLASS ORGANIZATION

Grouping: Groups of five or six students.
Time: 60 minutes.
Materials: None.

THE EXERCISE

1. Ask students to work in small groups of five or six. Each group makes two lists. The first contains the writing skills they need and the problems they think they face, and the second what they are prepared to do to improve in terms of class attendance, quality and quantity of work, independent follow-up, and commitment and application generally.
2. When the lists are complete, ask each group to write a contract letter to the tutor explaining what they hope to get from the course and what they will offer in terms of attendance, commitment, etc., in exchange for the tutor trying to meet their needs.

COMMENTS

Very often, especially in the sciences, students are required to contribute to collectively produced pieces of academic writing. This exercise focuses on two typical aspects of such writing:
- how a team of writers takes each different perspective into account and still produces something of substance;
- the notion of a *quid pro quo* or trade-off and how to describe it in writing.

It very often helps to discuss how a student from a different culture can contribute judgements to the discussion that produces this sort of writing and what role the student might have in the various stages of the writing process.

Acknowledgement: This idea is Denny Packard's, not ours.

Organization

4 Linking paragraphs

FOCUS

Although this exercise is called *Linking paragraphs*, it is really about the range of ways in which different approaches to a topic can be arranged in relation to each other. Learning to write is partly about learning how different kinds of information can be presented to the reader in a single essay. In common with several others, this exercise requires the same text to be worked over several times by a small group whose overt interest is in its meaning. The extent to which the accuracy of the writing is continuously improved during these various reworkings is usually very noticeable.

In Part 1 we described this exercise as seen from teacher and student perspectives in the classroom (see pp. 72–3).

CLASS ORGANIZATION

Grouping: This exercise works particularly well with large classes. The ideal size for each group is four, but where this is not possible threes are better than fives.

Time: 75 minutes.

Materials: Each student needs a small rectangular piece of card in one colour and a small circular piece of card in another. Spare pieces of circular card.

THE EXERCISE

1. Divide the class into groups of four. Each group should choose a different theme to write on. Possible themes include: family life in one's home country, marriage, if Marx had never lived, racism, a country in the news, learning English, a political controversy, sexism, etc. Once a group has chosen its theme, each member writes one paragraph on the theme on the rectangular card without liaising as to content with other members of the group.

2. When everyone in the group has written their paragraph the members of the group read each other's and decide how to order them relative to each other – i.e., what sort of logic will be needed to connect them together in a continuous piece of writing.

3. The group as a whole then writes linking passages to precede each

81

paragraph on their circular pieces of card. The whole text (i.e., linking passages and paragraphs) is then attached to the wall:

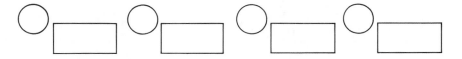

4. Once this has been done, the group reads the work of another group which is also on the wall. The idea is to 'spoil' the other group's work by putting a line through just one of their linking passages (i.e., through one of the links written on a circular piece of card). It is best to choose the linking passage most crucial to the argument.

5. As soon as a group sees a line has been put through one of its passages, it returns to base. This is when it is most helpful for the tutor to explain the next stage and to make clear that the logical idea contained in the passage struck out may not be used again – for example, if 'whilst' had been struck out, it couldn't be replaced by 'whereas'.

6. The group now reassembles its piece of writing with:
   – all the original paragraphs;
   – all the linking passages except the one struck out;
   – a replacement linking passage (so long as it does not contain the same logical idea as the one struck out).

   Very often it may be sensible to change the order in which the paragraphs are presented, and even sometimes to attach surviving linking passages to different paragraphs. The new arrangement is put up on the wall, and the group sets off again to 'spoil' another piece of writing.

7. Allow each group's work to be 'spoilt' three or four times before stopping the exercise. Groups may then like to have time to record successful sets of logical connections.

ILLUSTRATION

Here is an outcome that actually occurred with a group of three students writing about family life in their own countries (the linking passages are in italics):

It is instructive to examine the style of family life in a society that lives by traditional standards. So we find that

Family life in Libya is very simple. Extended families are existing in most places. Families are large, it is not surprising that the average size of the Libyan family is 5.9 persons. Men in most cases are the breadwinners and women are expected to bear and rear children besides the domestic work. However, in the last two decades so many changes have started to affect the family life environment. Women began to participate in the labour force and the intricate social structure is disturbed.

A comparable situation, but one which is perceived as less acceptable exists elsewhere in Africa. Thus

Family life in Ethiopia leaves much to be desired. This is mainly because the relationship that exists between a husband and wife is that of a master–servant relation. The only source of income is the husband. The main duty of the wife is restricted to what is taking place in the house and rearing children. The wife doesn't enjoy equal rights as the husband in the society at large.

On the other hand, there are considerable dangers in a too rapid change. For example,

The family life has ceased to exist in Germany. The children want to leave home very soon and many older people are left lonely. When people choose to marry, often divorce becomes more common.

When *On the other hand . . .* was struck out, the reassembled essay took the following form: *It is generally agreed that . . .* The family life has ceased . . . *At the same time, it is instructive . . .* Family life in Libya . . . *A comparable situation . . .* Family life in Ethiopia . . .

COMMENTS

This same exercise can be used from time to time with the same class. The more a class practises it, the better they get at connecting their arguments together, and the better they get at spotting cheating – i.e., the same logical idea being recycled in a new form.

As an out-of-class activity ask students to take an article or chapter from a textbook and look first at the ordering of the paragraphs. They should then look carefully at any linking devices that relate one paragraph to another or to the central thread of the argument. Next ask them to analyse a second chapter or article and compare the ordering and linking techniques of the two passages. Finally, the students should be asked to look at a recent example of their own work and decide what lessons they can learn from this activity for their next writing assignment.

Acknowledgement: Much of this exercise was put together by Edzard Gunther, Hu Xiao-ling, T S Mathula, Raphik Ovasapians and Tensay Woldesenbet as part of an EAP project on their MA in Applied Linguistics course at Durham.

5   Generalization

FOCUS

This exercise explores ways of picking out and presenting the most general information from a variety of items that range from the general to the highly specific. One of the real difficulties when doing this in writing is that generalization is often associated with relatively undisciplined talk. For that reason, in the exercise that follows, learners have an opportunity to contrast three contexts in which generalization might occur:
– the informal face-to-face context;
– the more formal spoken context;
– the written context.

CLASS ORGANIZATION

Grouping: This exercise is best divided between sessions (preferably, but not necessarily, consecutive classes). In the first session, learners work in pairs gathering information to present in diagrammatic form to their colleagues. In the second, students work in small groups with the aim of rejoining the whole class to share their work and discuss outcomes. An ideal class size is fifteen to twenty.

Time: First session: up to 60 minutes; second session: up to 75 minutes.

Materials: First session: card, felt pens; second session: cassette recorder and (if available) video camera.

THE EXERCISE

In the first session, ask the students to work in pairs. Using the rest of the class as informants, each pair should choose one topic of investigation. Suitable topics include family size, television preferences, eating habits, state of health, political attitudes, etc. It is important to ensure that each pair chooses a different topic.

The purpose is to collect as much information as possible and present it in diagrammatic form (e.g., graph, bar-chart, pie-chart, Venn diagram, grid, table, or flow chart). The results should be clearly presented on card and pinned to the wall.

For the second session, students should work in groups of three to five on a presentation entitled: 'The typical member of our class'. There must be a least three groups, one working towards each of the following outcomes:
– a relaxed style spoken presentation – on video where possible;
– a radio style documentary presentation on cassette;
– a journal style written report.
Each group should select and present only the most general information collected in the first session. With larger classes, two or more groups can work on the same style of presentation.

After the presentations, there should be a class discussion of the different language and level of formality appropriate to each presentation. The teacher's views on the presentations and general guidance will obviously help the students.

COMMENTS

1. If you have a video camera, it is useful to record the presentation stage in the second session and make the tape available for independent viewing.
2. The differences in register to which this exercise draws attention seem much more arbitrary to a second language learner than to a native speaker. Raising learners' awareness of the importance of being able to present the same information differently and appropriately in different contexts is very important.
3. Suggest that students prepare for one of their forthcoming lectures by reading a chapter or an article on the lecture topic, noting the way in which generalizations are made in the writing. They are then in a position to notice how differently the same material is handled in a lecture, and should be prepared to discuss these differences in a future class. This activity also provides a useful technique for making listening to lectures more productive for the student.

6   The use of illustrative examples

FOCUS

If someone writes a sentence like, 'It is usually surprisingly difficult for an adult to write fluently in a foreign language', most people will agree. They do not need to illustrate the point with an example to convince the reader. But a writer who never, or very rarely, uses illustrative examples, is typically less persuasive as a result.

This exercise is about the judicious use of illustrative examples. It offers students the chance to judge the quality and appropriacy of illustrative examples for themselves.

CLASS ORGANIZATION

Grouping: Students work in groups of four or five.
Time: Approximately 60 minutes, depending on class size.
Materials: One large envelope for each group.

THE EXERCISE

1. Each group should decide on a topic of interest to themselves, such as language learning, food and eating, injustice, the family, political extremism, the opposite sex, houses or whatever. Once the topic has

been chosen, the group should collectively write a short passage (approximately eight sentences in length) on their topic, but without giving any examples.

2. Each short passage is then passed from one group to another, together with a large envelope. The groups decide on two places in each text they receive where the insertion of an example would be appropriate. These places, and the actual examples to be inserted, should be indicated on a separate sheet of paper, which is put into the envelope and is not to be studied by the next group on the circuit. Continue this activity until all the groups have worked on all the passages.

3. Finally, the passages (and the accompanying envelopes) are returned to the authoring groups, who decide which illustrative examples they wish to incorporate into their texts. When they have done this, the rewritten texts can be displayed on the wall.

COMMENTS

As a follow-up activity, you can ask students to read their last assignment through and evaluate it for use of illustrations. Were there too many or too few? How appropriate were they? Students should also be asked to read a chapter or an article and to pick out the illustrative examples, deciding which are helpful in clarifying or adding interest and which are not. Sometimes it is difficult to distinguish a practical example that is actually being discussed as an integral part of a piece of writing from an example that is used illustratively. If this is so, it is helpful to talk through an example of each before or after the students embark on this reading.

7   Inserting additional material

FOCUS

We quite often find ourselves with an apparently finished piece of writing and then suddenly come across something additional we want to include. This exercise aims to make students aware of the options in this area – of how and where to insert new material and of the need to watch out for any consequential changes.

CLASS ORGANIZATION

Grouping: Students should work in pairs.

Time: 45 minutes.

Materials: This exercise must follow on from an exercise in which students have each produced extended paragraphs or essays on the same or a similar topic. Several of the exercises in this book are suitable. Alternatively, it can be used with students who have all written the same assignments in their subject class.

THE EXERCISE

1. Ask students to work in pairs. Paired students should exchange their pieces of writing and underline one sentence in their partner's passage which contains an idea that they would like to insert appropriately into their own writing. Each pair should end up with two passages (A & B) with one sentence in each underlined. The idea contained in the underlined sentence of the A passage is to be incorporated into the B passage, and vice versa.
2. The two passages should be exchanged for another pair's passages. Each pair now tries to accomplish the two insertion tasks it has been handed.

COMMENTS

1. If you want to provide more writing practice for your students after step three, ask each pair to return the suggested rewrites to the original authors. The original passages should be exchanged for a further pair's passages, and the insertion tasks attempted for a second time. This further option makes a good homework task.
2. The ability to insert new or original material is a very important rewriting skill. It often helps students to discuss the insertion process, i.e.:
   - how to recognize where to insert the new material;
   - in what form to insert it;
   - what large or small consequential changes to the original text are required.

   Students may also ask whether there are techniques for adding material without altering the existing text. This is an opportunity to discuss foot- and end-notes and other forms of addenda and to compare their effect with that of an integral insertion.
3. For students writing dissertations or theses, the discussion can include word processing options and/or strategies for handling the typing-up stage as well as ways of involving the supervisor in assisting with advice on the insertion of new material.

8 Ordering material

FOCUS

Everyone agrees that the way we order our material when we write is essential to our arguments. The decisions we need to take about the order of our material are often very difficult and time consuming. For this reason we may sometimes be reluctant to commit ourselves to the necessary hard work involved, and particularly when we are already facing the problems of working in a second language.

D

This exercise is likely to produce more than one possible ordering of material, together with a group of students ready to champion each possible ordering. Before we can order our material though, it needs to be classified. In this exercise, therefore, some preliminary classification is required.

CLASS ORGANIZATION

Grouping: Students begin working alone and then form small groups. A whole class decision is required half way through the small group phase. Finally, pairs of small groups team up. There is also the option of individual follow-up work.

Time: Upwards of 60 minutes.

Materials: None.

THE EXERCISE

1. Each student should list the letters he or she received on the last two days they were visited by the postman. Students then form groups which have received a total of approximately twenty letters and each group classifies these letters under as many headings as are appropriate.
2. The class then chooses (or is given) an essay title. Possible titles include: 'Letters – pleasurable or burdensome?', 'Do the advantages of receiving letters outweigh the disadvantages?', 'What do letters tell us about life?' The title should be the same for all the groups.
3. Once each group has the title, it can begin to plan an essay, deciding what arguments to use, how to order the different classes of letter and which particular letters to use to illustrate points. Do not rush this phase – encourage each group to reach a consensus that can be summarized in an essay plan, which the group should write down.
4. When a group finishes, pair them up with another group. Each group should explain their own essay plan and discuss the relative strengths and weaknesses of each other's decisions.
5. Now that the essay has been planned, it can always, of course, be written. This makes a good voluntary homework task for those who want the maximum amount of writing practice.

COMMENTS

One way of extending this is to ask students to discuss the relevance of this exercise to essay writing in their own main subjects:

— To what extent do they see essay based tutorial work as centred on how to order information?
— Can anyone talk through an essay currently being planned?
— What conventional ordering of the main elements do students expect to find in essays, dissertations, or academic papers?

9 Structuring paragraphs

FOCUS

Writers often have problems organizing ideas within a paragraph as well as within a longer stretch of writing. One problem, for example, is knowing when in the paragraph to make a generalization about a series of smaller points.

This exercise takes an unfortunate incident as its topic. It relies on the chronological order of events to demonstrate how the paragraph that describes the incident can be gradually more closely knit, and on a summing-up device to give a sense of coherence. The question of where best to place that summing-up device is also considered. Groups are encouraged to use different techniques to produce different types of paragraph.

CLASS ORGANIZATION

Grouping: Students must work in groups of four.
Time: 60 minutes.
Materials: A video recording if available.

THE EXERCISE

1. Choose a short video recording (i.e., not more than two minutes) of some unfortunate event (real or fictional) and play it to the class. Something as simple as an incident involving the police or some domestic misfortune is fine.

    The purpose of the video is to stimulate members of the class to focus on similar events in their own lives. Allow two or three minutes of silent thought time to recall such an incident.

    (If you do not have a video you can use an audio tape, tell a story or read a brief text.)
2. Divide the class into groups of four. Each group chooses the unfortunate event of one of its members to explore further. The group discuss and note down the sequence of events that led up to the incident. They then decide how to express the way the incident ended in a single sentence. This may be either a statement of fact, or its implications, or a judgement on it. The list of events and the single sentence must be agreed by all four in the group.
3. The groups then split into two pairs. One pair has the task of starting with the agreed sentence and describing the events leading up to it in any order so as to bring out causal or other relationships between them. The second pair works forward to the agreed sentence, which will appear as the final sentence, relating the chronologically ordered events to each other and, where possible, to the final outcome.
4. Pairs stick their paragraphs to the wall, with the two paragraphs from the same group side by side. Each pair evaluates all the paragraphs on

the wall, deciding in each case whether putting the outcome sentence first or last worked better with the material.

5. The class share their evaluations. They may also want to discuss the different types of writing that members of the class have to do in the real world to demonstrate how the same principles of structuring a paragraph might be useful.

COMMENTS

1. Instead of an unfortunate incident, this exercise might centre on the events leading up to a decisive moment in the life of a group member, e.g., going to live away from home, giving a public performance of some kind or getting married.

2. There are a number of important issues relating to paragraph structure which students often benefit from discussing in class. These include:
   - the relationship between the topic sentence of a paragraph and the other sentences;
   - whether there are differences between preferred paragraph structures in one academic subject and another. (How sure are students of their facts – should they go away and check their opinions against texts?);
   - whether other paragraph structures besides the ones practised in this session are found;
   - can they find a writer in their subject area whose paragraph structures might be considered exemplary?

3. Turning to their own writing, can your students evaluate how internally coherent the paragraphs in their last piece of writing were? And are their paragraphs too long, too short or about right?

10   Sub-headings: exercises A and B

FOCUS

A Ph.D. thesis one of us was recently involved in assessing was heavily criticized by one of the examiners for its lack of suitably numbered and underlined sub-headings. From the reader's point of view, it meant it was hard to find a way through an otherwise excellent piece of writing full of inventive ideas.

Even a quite modest assignment can be made more readable by the proper use of headings. The function of sub-headings is to signal the structure of a piece of writing. They typically take the form of phrases emphasized by spacing, numbering, position and underlining, or by one of these alternatives. We suggest two exercises of a similar kind to create awareness of the required skills.

CLASS ORGANIZATION

Grouping: For Exercise A the class works first in pairs and then individually; in Exercise B the class works first in small groups and then as a whole class.

Time: Exercise A: 60 minutes, Exercise B: 45 minutes.

Materials: Exercise A: outline form (see p. 92).

EXERCISE A

1. Seat the class in pairs. Each person should ask their partner about the subject discipline or profession their partner knows most about, and fill in the outline form for it as accurately as possible so as to show its major divisions.

   It is usually a good idea for the class to discuss a different topic first to illustrate the problems and methodology required. Sport works well as it can be divided in so many equally valid ways – ball/non-ball games, individual/team sports, etc. Ball games themselves can be subdivided into large and small ball games or into games where the ball is struck with an implement and those where it is not.

2. When the outlines are completed, they should be pinned to the wall. Working individually, each member of the class writes a single paragraph on one of the topics headlined in his or her outline, indicating how it relates to topics at the same level and to those at both deeper and shallower levels.

3. The paragraphs are collected by the teacher and redistributed so that everyone has someone else's. Students look at the outlines attached to the wall and try to identify which section of which outline is being described in the paragraph.

   The paragraph should be attached to the appropriate outline, together with any comments on how its relation to other headlined topics could have been made clearer by the original writer.

EXERCISE B

1. Ask the students to write any recent spelling mistakes they have made or come across in both corrected and uncorrected forms on the board.

2. In groups of three, the students try to decide on categories of spelling error, together with illustrative examples.

3. As a whole class, including the teacher, share some of the ways of categorizing spelling errors. Try to categorize types of error under headings and sub-headings.

4. As a homework task, each student should write a paragraph about the category of error they find most difficult to avoid. These paragraphs can be brought to class and stuck on a large teacher-made outline of categories of spelling error.

WORKSHEET: SUB-HEADINGS EXERCISE A

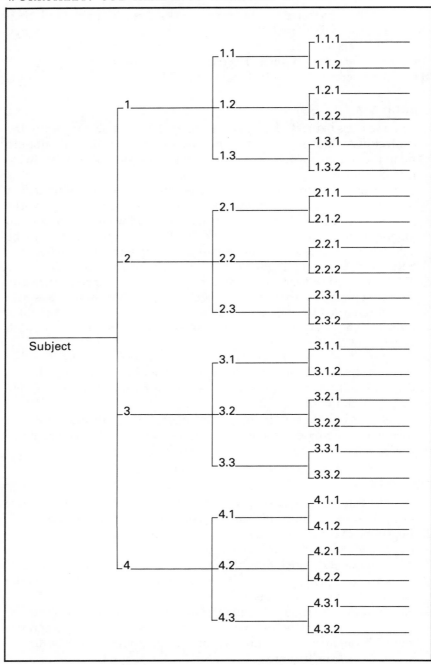

COMMENTS

Students from different subject departments may well be operating with widely differing 'house rules' in this area. An exchange of views on what is possible is a good idea. Other topics worth discussion include:
– how long a text needs to be for sub-headings to be required;
– what sort of information a sub-heading should contain and how it should relate to the text that follows;
– numbering possibilities for sub-headings;
– the relationship between sections and chapters, foot- and end-notes, references and the bibliography.

The sociology of writing

Observing cultural constraints

11 Using sources

FOCUS

Every culture has slightly different views on this topic. And sometimes cultures differ markedly. For example, native members of the British culture would typically agree that word-for-word copying out of un-acknowledged source material is totally unacceptable. On the other hand, there are societies in which the word-for-word reproduction of a university lecture is the safest way of ensuring success in the subsequent examination!

Broadly speaking, most users of English as first language feel that a limited quantity of direct quotation (i.e., using quotation marks), and a fairly close summary of original material which acknowledges its sources are appropriate in a more extensive piece of writing. Indeed, provided that such quotation and summary are acknowledged, they will lend weight to the opinions of the writer.

The aim of this exercise is to help students to become aware of the right balance between source material and their own views.

CLASS ORGANIZATION

Grouping: First lesson in pairs, second lesson in fours.

Time: One of the problems of this activity is that it tends to take different students different lengths of time to do the writing. A good solution is to start the writing phase in the last ten minutes of a session and have it completed for homework. If you adopt this strategy, the activity takes about thirty minutes at the end of one class and ten to fifteen minutes at the beginning of the next.

Materials: You will need a set of 200–400 word horoscopes for the students to consult. With larger classes you will need more than one horoscope for each star sign or Chinese year. Somerville, N., *Your Chinese Horoscope* and Crowmarsh, P., *First Steps in Astrology*, both Aquarius Press, contain suitable material.

THE EXERCISE

1. Ask students to pair themselves with a fellow student who is not a close friend but to whom they feel they can talk openly. Give each student ten minutes to try to assess what sort of a person their partner is by asking questions about life style, work, habits, outlook, attitudes, moods, preferences, etc. The questioner should keep careful notes as they will be needed later to write from.

2. When the twenty minutes are over, make the horoscopes available.

   At this stage, each student therefore has their own assessment of a colleague's personality, and the horoscope in front of them. Before starting to write, each student needs to spend two or three minutes deciding how to use the horoscope:
   – does it support their conclusions?
   – does it supplement them?
   – does it contradict them?

   Each student now writes a short personality profile of their partner based on what they discovered when asking their partner questions and on the horoscope for their partner's birth sign, which should be quoted from word for word, and summarized, in both cases with acknowledgement.

   The writing phase should be completed for homework.

3. At the beginning of the next class, ask each of the original pairs to team up with a second pair of students to form a group of four. They should exchange profiles, and evaluate how successful each of the four writers has been in using their source material.

COMMENTS

When discussing the use of sources, questions worth raising include:
– What are the received attitudes to using sources in the students' own culture(s)?
– What are the received attitudes to the use of sources in the host country? What ethical considerations are present? What penalties can ensue if the conventions are ignored?
– For students studying overseas, what difficulties have they encountered in the host culture with the use of sources and what advice has been given, directly or indirectly, by tutors or supervisors?
– To what extent, and in what parts of a piece of work, is reference to sources favoured/required?
– What part does reference to sources play in the information structure of a piece of academic writing?
– What sort of punctuation, layout and foot- or end-note techniques are required for direct quotation?
– What referencing techniques are usual?
– How close to the original should a paraphrase or summary be?

– Is it ever permissible not to acknowledge derived material? What counts as 'derived material'?

Students can be asked to read an academic paper in their own subject area and study its use of sources.

12   Entering caveats

FOCUS

Many of us from time to time have difficulty deciding how to say things about which we are less than certain but which we nevertheless want to say. If we are working with a second language, we will expect to find this still more difficult. And as we write for a more and more sophisticated audience, we need to be even more sophisticated in the way we enter our caveats. So while an intermediate level learner may find 'seem' or 'appear' and the occasional 'although' clause adequate to hedge his or her opinions, the advanced learner will require a far more extensive repertoire.

This exercise aims to highlight the difference between what we are certain of and what we are less certain of in a particular area. It then explores ways of indicating varying degrees of uncertainty.

CLASS ORGANIZATION

Grouping: This exercise begins with a class brainstorm, then draws on individual knowledge, before grouping the students in threes for the writing task. Groups are asked to evaluate their colleagues' work.

Time: 60 minutes.

Materials: Several small pieces of paper.

THE EXERCISE

1. Have the class imagine themselves as Martians and brainstorm as many as possible of the obvious ways a Martian would recognize the differences between summer and winter in Britain. (We use Britain throughout this exercise and elsewhere in the book – the country where you are situated and its seasonal variations can obviously be substituted.)

2. Next, ask the class to work individually. Ask them to write down suggested answers to your questions about the differences between summer and winter in Britain, to which they may well not know the answers. Possible questions might include:

   – How, if at all, does the typical British breakfast differ in summer and winter?

   – Are there particular months in which British people typically stop. and restart wearing vests?

   – Do politicians tend to favour winter or summer for general elections?

- In which months, if any, do British people not mow their lawns?
- Do British people tend to go to bed earlier in summer or winter?
- Would you expect the British to use their cars more in summer or winter?
- Are more British babies born in summer or winter?

Finally, each student should think up two or three differences for themselves.

3. Group the students in threes and ask them to compare answers.

Each group should choose something they are (a) relatively sure of, (b) half certain of, and (c) pretty doubtful about.

Then they should write single sentences stating their views with due caution on three separate small pieces of paper labelled (a), (b) and (c) on the reverse side. These pieces of paper should be pinned to the wall in random order with the sentence side displayed, and then other groups should decide whether they are in the right or wrong order.

COMMENTS

1. After the exercise, it is usually a good idea to encourage students to make a vocabulary guide of ways of hedging an opinion or entering a caveat in each of the three categories of sentence displayed.
2. If you are working with a mixed nationality group, it is also possible to get the students to supply the questions. Each student asks one question about their own country.
3. A follow-up discussion might focus on whether it is a strength or a weakness to admit to uncertainty in writing, and on how uncertain one can be and still make the point. If the students (and the tutor) have early and later drafts of a piece of writing where the expression of tentativeness varies, they can bring them to class for discussion.
4. As a follow-up activity, ask each student to find three caveats from a chapter or article they have been reading to bring to class. These can be shared in a class discussion based on the degree of tentativeness demonstrated by each example.

13 Using counter-arguments

FOCUS

In chapter 2 we suggested a cultural difference between those who suppress any counter-arguments to the main thesis on the assumption that they weaken that thesis and those who think that their hand is strengthened by showing an awareness of counter-arguments (even if sometimes of minor importance).

In this exercise, students are asked to put their own strongly held counter-arguments to an equally strongly held thesis expressed by a fellow student. They therefore need to argue tactfully if they are to persuade.

CLASS ORGANIZATION

Grouping: Students work as individuals.

Time: This exercise needs three short classroom sessions on successive days (perhaps five, fifteen and thirty minutes). The writing will be completed as two overnight homework tasks.

Materials: Access to a photocopier.

THE EXERCISE

1. In the first session, ask each student to write a one page statement on a self-selected issue about which they feel particularly strongly. Encourage students to choose issues like the punishment of offenders, religious belief, nuclear power, censorship. These statements should be completed as a homework task and brought to the next day's class.
2. In the second session, attach three copies of each piece of homework to the wall and allow students fifteen minutes to read all the statements. Each student then selects one with which they strongly disagree and removes it from the wall.
3. This statement should be taken as a definitive view to be cited and argued against tactfully in a piece of writing to be completed as a homework task and brought to class the following day.
4. In the third session, the original statements together with the counter-arguments should be put up on the wall to stimulate discussion of the language of counter-argument. A vocabulary guide may be made.

COMMENTS

When one writes, the problem is sometimes one of handling counter-arguments and sometimes one of handling counter-evidence.

Counter-arguments: Ask students to supply a piece of academic writing in their own subject area to see to what extent positions are established because the writer wishes to argue against them. In circumstances where there are two genuinely viable positions, what strategies does the writer use? How successfully were counter-arguments handled in the students' last piece of writing? To what extent does their subject department value the ability to put a counter thesis, as reflected in exam questions, essay titles, etc?

Counter-evidence: This problem occurs particularly in the sciences. Ask students to study an academic paper in their subject area to see where such evidence is suppressed and where it is admitted; they should observe whether the counter-evidence is presented first or second and what devices are used to diminish its impact.

14 'I' in formal writing

FOCUS

Not all non-native users of English have the same view of the use of the first person pronoun in formal writing as native writers seem to have.

EAP teachers, for example, will be familiar with the 'I' dominated essay, where very often 'I' is used to introduce those parts of the work that a student wishes to show off as generalities thought up by the author – the this-is-important I, if you like. In the formal writing of native speakers, however, there turns out to be a close association of 'I' with 'although' and tentative expressions like 'tend to think', 'would be inclined to doubt', etc. In these contexts, 'I' seems to be used as a functional demur – a very different purpose from that for which some overseas students use it.

Although 'I' is associated with other contexts too (for example, as a signpost – 'I wish next to consider...'), this exercise concentrates on the tentative or demurring use of I.

The aim of the exercise is to provide a context in which, firstly, the students feel they are writing formally (they must refer to themselves by their full names), and in which subsequently they feel justified in using 'I' to cast just a shade of doubt on someone else's claim about themselves.

CLASS ORGANIZATION

Grouping: Students will move around the classroom individually. The bigger the class the better.
Time: Up to 60 minutes.
Materials: None.

THE EXERCISE

1. Ask each student to take a sheet of paper and write a single sentence describing something they did, achieved or that happened to them. It should be something out of the ordinary which, although true, might be greeted with surprise. In this sentence, they should refer to themselves by their full names. Thus we could produce the following sentences:

   'Arthur Edgar Brookes once found himself teaching an exam class in geography, though it was a subject he'd never studied beyond the age of ten himself.'
   'There was an occasion when Peter Grundy paraded as a male model at a fashion show in front of a hundred champagne swilling socialites.'

2. These sheets should be left on the desks. The students then move around the classroom adding a doubt expressing sentence containing 'I' to as many of the sheets of paper as time allows.

COMMENTS

The next time the students read a learned article, encourage them to look for examples of the demurring 'I' and decide how they are used and whether they are effective. Students can also bring to class the other varieties of 'I' they find in written texts. If you judge it right, the discussion can also be broadened to include the place of 'we' in academic writing.

15   Promoting nominal style

FOCUS

Most writers want to persuade their readers of a point of view. There is a conventional way of doing this in academic English that many second language users do not always fully understand.

When we write an essay, we typically begin by reviewing what is already known in the field, and only after we have done that do we introduce our own new, or modifying, ideas. This information structure is found everywhere – in essays, papers and articles. Even individual sentences typically begin with a topic or subject known to both reader and writer, which is then commented on in the predicate, or second part, of the sentence. The word 'the' in English partly functions to remind us that the noun phrase in which it occurs refers to some event, object, person or idea already known to both speaker/writer and hearer/reader.

If you look carefully at the writing of language learners, you will very often find that they pay too little attention to established knowledge and are too quick to try and sell their own ideas to the reader. This is often marked by the use of 'a'/'an' in noun phrases in the opening sentences of their writing in places where a native speaker would prefer 'the'.

We have noticed these problems so often in our own students' work that we have invented the exercise that follows to help language learners to understand the typical information structure of an English sentence, which begins with a known subject or topic, and then goes on to say something new about it.

CLASS ORGANIZATION

Grouping: Groups of six work best, but fives or sevens are also possible.
Time: At least 45 minutes.
Materials: Several half sheets of paper per student.

THE EXERCISE

1. Ask the students to close their eyes and call to mind a time when they quite consciously decided to experiment (preferably successfully) with

a changed life style (e.g., by giving up smoking, trying to get on with someone, etc.).

2. A volunteer describes their experience concisely, and immediately afterwards each member of the group writes down their own response in the form: 'a/an ... (supply modifiers) ... experience which ... (complete relative clause but do not write a full sentence)...'

   It is as well to check that each student in the group has done the right thing, so perhaps you might share your phrase at this stage, which should look something like this: 'An interesting and rather unexpected experience which did ultimately demonstrate that women probably are more intelligent than men...' The precise content of your sentence will, of course, depend on what the experience actually was.

3. Call for a second volunteer to describe their experience, and again each member of the group writes down a response in the 'a/an ... experience which...' form. It is important that each response is written down on a new piece of paper.

   Call for other volunteers and continue writing response statements until everyone in the group has described their experience.

4. Instruct each student to replace all the initial indefinite articles with 'the' or 'this'. (E.g., 'An interesting and rather unexpected...' becomes 'The interesting and rather unexpected...')

5. Instruct the students to complete the five or so sentences whose subjects only they have written down so far. The next three words they write should be '...reminds me of...' Again, it may be helpful to share your example: 'The interesting and rather unexpected experience which did ultimately demonstrate that women probably are more intelligent than men reminds me of the time my mother-in-law successfully persuaded my father-in-law that a course of dog vitamin pills would cure his baldness.'

   As each sentence is completed, it should be passed to the person whose experience it refers to.

COMMENTS

1. This exercise quite often results in slightly exaggerated examples of the right sort of opening sentence. It sometimes helps to introduce some authentic examples after the students have completed their writing.

2. In some countries, this rather ponderous style is fairly typical of an educated native speaker writing for non-academic purposes. Often learners of English have been told to avoid it when writing English. Under these circumstances, one will need to discuss the differences between the usual more verbal style and what is acceptable and indeed expected in a more academic context.

3. In order to reinforce the point made in this exercise, ask your students to review their most recent academic writing, even to bring it to class – they will be sure to find a large proportion of the opening sentences of their work get this one wrong.

   It is also worth discussing the psychological difficulty of using these devices, which essentially bring the writer and reader closer together, when the writer is working in a foreign language (and perhaps culture) and does not feel particularly close to the native speaker of English who is also a teacher or supervisor.

   You can also ask your students to search out model opening sentences in academic articles and textbooks.

16   Question or statement?

FOCUS

Many students have a natural tendency to write a question into an essay as a kind of signal that the writer needs to pause to think out the answer, which may, with luck, appear in the following sentence. For obvious reasons, this is not the most effective use of direct or indirect questions in writing. But just what function do questions have in a continuous piece of writing?

This exercise firstly generates a set of questions (e.g., 'What would you take with you if you ran away?') and answers (e.g., 'I'd take a television set') for each student. Then each student decides which of the original set of questions might retain its question form in a continuous piece of writing that is essentially made up of the set of answers.

CLASS ORGANIZATION

Grouping: Each student first completes a questionnaire alone. Working with two different partners, each student discusses their own question-naire and that of one of their partners. Finally, each student writes individually. Where there is an odd number of students in the class, the teacher should join in.

Time: At least 75 minutes.

Materials: Two copies of the questionnaire per student (see p. 103).

THE EXERCISE

1. Give an Escapes questionnaire to each student for completion. This can be a pre-class activity.
2. When the questionnaires are completed, pair the students. One is to act as interviewer and one as interviewee. Give a second questionnaire sheet to the interviewer who should complete this with the information elicited from the interviewee about his or her escape.

WORKSHEET: ESCAPES QUESTIONNAIRE

ESCAPES

1. Where would you go? Why?

2. Who, if anyone, would you take with you? Who, if anyone, would you hope to meet there? Why?

3. What, if anything, would you take with you? Why?

4. Which friends, if any, would you keep in touch with? Why?

5. Which members of your family, if any, would you keep in touch with? Why?

6. If you could do one dishonest thing and get away with it, what would it be? Why?

7. Which book, if any, would you take with you? Why?

8. What would you look for in your new life? Why?

9. In what major ways would you want your new life to be different from your present one? Why?

10. Do you believe it would work? Would you be happier?

Encourage the interviewers to let the interviewees talk freely – i.e., supplementary or elucidatory questions are very much to be encouraged.

3. When the interviews are completed, students form new pairs. Former interviewers now become interviewees, and vice versa. Distribute second questionnaires to the interviewers and repeat the stage two process.

4. By now, each student should have a completed questionnaire summarizing the escape of another member of the class.

   Students now work individually, writing a short description and evaluation of their classmate's escape and deciding in which one or two places to use a direct or indirect question rather than a statement.

5. When the writing phase is over the students reassemble, first in pairings as at stage two and then in pairings as at stage three to read their passages to their partners and explain why they decided to use direct or indirect questions where they actually did.

COMMENTS

1. We have found that this exercise works best when the idea of escape is thought about realistically rather than romantically. Sometimes it helps to have a short warm-up exercise designed to reinforce the more realistic aspects of starting a new life. For example, the cartoon below works well if used as a jigsaw: make enough copies for each learner to get a quarter of the whole cartoon once you have cut it into exactly equal quarters. (We usually cut it diagonally from corner to corner.) Group the learners in fours so that each member of the group has a different quarter. Each student then describes their part of the cartoon to the other members of the group – the purpose is for the group as a whole to 'get the joke'.

2. When they write many students who follow lecture courses tend to

imitate the lecturing style that favours asking questions as a preliminary to giving information. Discuss the reasons why this may be a good lecturing technique but is not necessarily appropriate in writing.

The following questions lead to a productive discussion:
- What principles for using questions emerged in this exercise?
- How do you use questions in your main subject work?
- When a question occurs in an article or textbook, how many sentences or pages does it normally take to answer it? In what sort of ways and over what expanse of discourse is the question referred to subsequently?

If the use of rhetorical questions emerges during the discussion, the different proportions of these in written and spoken language can be discussed.

Writing for a purpose

17 Writing a forecast

FOCUS

In many formal writing contexts it is necessary to make a forecast based on information currently available. This exercise aims to draw students' attention to the degrees of tentativeness which need to be employed to describe progressively more remote future possibilities.

CLASS ORGANIZATION

Grouping: Groups of five or six.
Time: 60–75 minutes.
Materials: None.

THE EXERCISE

1. Each student lists the first six things they would do if they became dictator of the world tomorrow.
2. Working in groups of five or six, each group listens to the dictats of all its members and then decides which particular student's dictatorial aspirations to work with.
3. The two questions each group should then consider are what short-term and what longer-term forecasts it is possible to make for the world given the six changes proposed. The group then works towards producing a two or three paragraph agreed prognosis.

COMMENTS

A possible follow-up is to collect in the forecasts and photocopy two or three of them together with lists of the six changes underlying each. These copies are then distributed to members of the class, who make adjustments to them so as to bring the forecasts into line with their own views. This rewriting phase helps to highlight the options in forecast writing.

Raising the awareness of students as to the different attitudes to describing prediction and forecast appropriate at the different stages in their research is one important application of this exercise.

Most students writing theses will be trying to prove a set of implicationally related hypotheses. Typically an element of supposition or forecasting enters into stating what it is hoped that the research will prove. Supervisors often encourage students to make these forecasts relatively tentatively in the early stages of a research project so that, as some are proved and others fail, those of the original working hypotheses that are proved can be rewritten less tentatively. Sometimes in writing the final chapter of a thesis in which implications are traced out and predictions made, a similarly tentative style will need to be adopted for describing possible future research findings.

Students in academic disciplines where forecast writing is prominent should study the linguistic features of forecasts written in their own disciplines. This is very important in some areas of business studies and economics.

18   How does an abstract differ from a summary?

FOCUS

This exercise demonstrates how abstracts and summaries differ. Most of us who read or write at all seriously will need to make effective written summaries of some of the texts we encounter. And for the convenience of our own potential readers, we will also need to produce brief abstracts of the texts for which we are responsible.

In a sense, the aim of this exercise is to draw attention to features of summary making and abstract writing by defining them in relation to each other – a 'definition by contraries' if you like.

CLASS ORGANIZATION

Grouping: Pairs.
Time: The exercise takes up to 90 minutes, which can be split into two parts: summary making, which comes first and takes about an hour, and abstract writing, which follows and takes about half an hour.
Materials: Each student must bring their homework and each pair will need a copy of the tutor's homework.

THE EXERCISE

Each student, and the tutor, must bring to class a piece of their own writing on a previously agreed theme. The passage should cover one side of A4. Collect this homework in. It is important to choose a theme where the teacher's views are expected to be different from those of the students, who in their turn may be expected to take up reasonably comparable positions. Good themes for students working in Britain include learning English, living in Britain, Northern Ireland, British people, shopping in Britain, British education or the Prime Minister. If you are not a British teacher or if your target variety is not British English, you will probably wish to choose a theme of comparable local relevance.

1. Pair students and ask them to decide whether, if they were given the views of two fellow students and their tutor on the given topic, they would expect the three views to be equally diverse or whether they would expect the two students' views to be closer to each other.

2. Distribute the pieces of writing around the class so that each pair receives two passages written by other members of the class and a copy of your own writing.

3. Pairs should first produce note form summaries of each piece of writing on the reverse side of each sheet. From these notes, each pair writes an 80–100 word summary in which the similarities and differences of view between one student and another and between tutor and students are brought out.

4. Each pair now writes an 80–100 word abstract stating what they set out to show/expected to find, the extent to which they were successful, and the method of work employed.

5. It is a good idea to let students circulate for ten minutes at the end so they can track down their own homework and see what was written about it, in the process reading other pairs' summaries and abstracts.

COMMENTS

Learners should be encouraged to study abstracts and summaries of articles in their fields of interest to see to what extent the authors observe the points that emerged in this exercise. Do abstracts typically follow the three part structure practised in this session? What other structures occur? What is the ideal length for an abstract of an article or of a thesis? When students read abstracts, what particularly do they expect them to contain? Can the students compile a list of typical defining properties of (a) abstracts and (b) summaries?

19   The written evaluation

FOCUS

It is always easy to talk informally of improving one thing or another, or to say that in general we are impressed with something. But when it comes to evaluating a situation in writing, we tend to hesitate. We think that this is partly because all too often we do not know exactly enough just what we are to write about and so in this exercise we take care to delimit the situation to be written about very carefully.

The exercise involves the evaluation of one student's situation by another, and the submission of a written evaluation at the end of the process.

CLASS ORGANIZATION

Grouping: Pairs.

Time: Up to 60 minutes. Alternatively, the writing up of the evaluation can be done as a homework task, in which case a twenty minute information gathering phase at the end of one lesson and a ten minute evaluation exchange at the beginning of the next day's work is adequate.

Materials: None.

THE EXERCISE

1. Pair students and ask them to interview each other. The purpose of the interview is to discover exactly what would happen if an emergency arose and the interviewee was to return as directly and speedily as possible, by public transport, to their home in whatever country or area they come from.

   When interviewing, each student should note down their partner's precise travel times and modes of transport, together with predictions about delays, time spent queuing, waiting, etc., and inquire carefully as to how efficient or satisfactory the traveller feels the arrangements to be.

2. Working with their colleague's travel outline, each student should then write an evaluation of the outline, drawing attention to those aspects of the schedule in need of improvement and those which are acceptable or even commendable. The evaluation should be presented to the student concerned.

COMMENTS

In some academic disciplines, students are trained to write evaluations of proposals, projects, work experience, and so on. Striking the right balance between being positive and critical and choosing the appropriate, objective language are both very problematical, especially for a second

language user. Questions you might want to ask in a follow-up discussion include:
- How does the experience of this exercise relate to the guidance provided in the subject department?
- In this exercise, how do students react to receiving evaluations and what causes these reactions?

20   Impersonal writing and probability

FOCUS

When one thinks about it, it is obvious that when we start sentences with 'I', we typically want to talk, or write, about things we have done. Therefore, it follows that a natural first step on the road to impersonal writing, which may be a necessary genre for some writing tasks, is to learn to write about things over which we, as individuals, have less control. This exercise is about separating the world into the things we might either predict or get to know on the one hand (i.e., sentences where we want to use 'I'), and the things that happen or just *are* despite ourselves on the other (i.e., sentences where impersonal writing feels more natural). Thus it would be natural to say, or write, 'Although *I predicted* the dictator's downfall, *it was impossible to foresee* the events which followed.'

Notice that impersonal writing, as the term is used here, describes sentences beginning with expressions like: 'It was impossible (for anyone) to tell...', 'It is highly unlikely that...', 'There is very little likelihood of/that...', 'If anyone had predicted x, it would have been...', 'That x remained undetected/unforeseen...', 'That x happened amazed me...', 'No one could have...', 'The fact that...' and passive sentences.

CLASS ORGANIZATION

Grouping: Students should work in groups of four, five or six. If you intend to do the follow-up activity, even numbers are required.
Time: 60 minutes.
Materials: None.

THE EXERCISE

1. Each student in the class should privately rearrange the contents of their pockets, handbags, wallets, etc., so that in one particular pocket there are:
   - five category A objects, i.e., objects that one might expect fellow students to guess successfully;
   - one category B object, i.e., an object that one's fellow students would be unlikely to predict was in one's pocket.

2. Ask students to form groups of five or six. Next each student lists five objects in category A (i.e., objects fellow students might be expected to have in their pockets), and five objects in category B (i.e., objects they think fellow students do actually have in their pockets but which are difficult to predict).

3. Each student in the group then reveals the contents of their pocket. Each of the other students makes a list of all the objects revealed that they failed to predict, with the name of the revealing student beside each one.

4. Each student then reorders their list of the objects that they failed to predict so that the most difficult object to guess is at the top and the least difficult at the bottom. An appropriate impersonal sentence should then be written for each object. For example: 'That Mahmoud turned out to have a dead beetle in his pocket astonished me'; or 'There was a good chance of predicting that Nourah had a cheque card in her pocket'.

COMMENTS

1. As a rewriting activity, it works well to ask pairs of students in the same group to integrate their answers, i.e., to combine their two separate lists of sentences. This involves first ranking the objects for degree of predictability and then ensuring that the sentences reflect this accurately, making minor alterations where necessary.

2. It may help to consider the sentence, 'It was possible to predict the dictator's downfall' from a more theoretical standpoint. According to Grice's theory of implicature (which is to do with how we understand ideas that are implied rather than explicitly stated), this sentence will usually imply that the speaker did not personally predict the dictator's downfall. This is because, if the speaker had predicted it, the less marked sentence, 'I predicted the dictator's downfall' would have been used instead. Some but not all implicatures of this kind cross cultural and linguistic boundaries.

   With suitable students it is worth discussing such sentences and their implicatures: it seems to be the case for many varieties of English that impersonal sentences do give rise to an implicature that the speaker or writer is not the initiator of the action described in the sentence: perhaps this is why we think of writing that contains impersonal structures as 'formal'.

   It is also important for students to understand that 'It was impossible to predict the dictator's downfall' is not in free variation with 'I didn't predict the dictator's downfall' and that in academic writing the impersonal sentence of the first type is preferred.

21 Records and reports

FOCUS

When we use writing to persuade (as discussed on pp. 14–16 in Part 1) then one very interesting writing moment will be the one at which we switch from writing for ourselves, as in keeping our own factual records, to reporting these to others. Should a report give prominence to particular elements, for example? Should it try to reach conclusions? To make connections? Or should a report simply record everything? The aim of this exercise is to explore the different views of report writing that inevitably surface when different writers are at work.

CLASS ORGANIZATION

This exercise requires the keeping of an orderly record for a week as a preparatory, homework activity.

Grouping: In class, students write in pairs since this helps to promote the impersonal presentation that is a typical feature of report writing.

Time: 60–75 minutes.

Materials: None.

THE EXERCISE

Instruct students to spend ten minutes on waking each morning making an exact record of their sleeping patterns during the preceding night. This should include length of sleep, whether continuous or intermittent, nature and causes of any interruption, times of going to bed, falling asleep, waking and getting up, whether dreams are recalled or not and subject-matter of those recalled, information gleaned from any room-mate as to snoring, sleep walking, talking in sleep, etc., as well as all other relevant facts (e.g., cheese at midnight, close weather).

This record should be brought to class on a prearranged day, the same lesson the following week is a good idea. In class:

1. Pair students and ask them to choose one of the two records in front of them to write about. The writing task is to turn this record into a report for a research project on sleeping patterns. Try not to be at all explicit as to how this report is to be written – what will be interesting will be the decisions each pair takes.
2. When the reports are written, ask each pair to exchange both record and report with another pair, who then try to identify the ways in which the report differs from the record.
3. Often it is a good idea to ask pairs either to present a brief evaluation of the report they have been reading to the whole class or to team up again with the pair with whom they had exchanged reports to discuss the findings. The former works well with small classes and the latter is better with large classes.

111

COMMENTS

1. This exercise may be compared with exercise 22 (*Report writing*), which works in a broadly similar way, but with a much more diffuse data set.
2. Turning to the wider applicability of this exercise, it will have obvious importance for research students who are encouraged to keep meticulous records as they collect their data. After the data are analysed, there will be an important chapter to write for the thesis reporting the data collection procedure and the findings. To what extent would the decisions taken in this exercise be appropriate in the students' academic disciplines? What linguistic strategies were used to highlight important or play down unimportant elements of the record?

   When students study the reports of earlier research in their own fields, is it possible to deduce how the researchers turned the records they kept into the reports they wrote?

22   Report writing

FOCUS

It would be mistaken to expect anything very original in the framework or style of a laboratory report or a routine maintenance report. We would concede that imitating a model may be the best way to learn to write such conventional reports, but very often much more latitude is allowed. If, for example, you were asked to report on a visit to another firm or institution, you would probably be expected to find a framework and style suitable for the content and audience.

The aim of this exercise is to give practice in report writing in a context where the framework is far from predetermined but where the class as a whole constitutes a well understood audience.

CLASS ORGANIZATION

Grouping: Whole class activity followed by group work.
Time: At least 90 minutes. Although it can be divided between two sessions, momentum is rapidly lost if different parts of the exercise take place on different days.
Materials: Realia – about twice as many small objects as there are students. Suitable objects include items of food, fruit, vegetables, buttons, coins, curios, small containers, postcards, flowers, articles of clothing, small toys and exotica; comment sheets; audio or video equipment (optional).

THE EXERCISE

1. Ask each student to choose one of the small objects at random. Allow

a five minute silent period in which each student tries to associate his or her object with a memory, perhaps from the recent or distant past, perhaps often recalled or until now forgotten. It will usually be helpful for students to make brief notes.

2. Ask as many students as are willing and as time allows to share these memories with their colleagues. The other students should listen carefully and take notes.

   If the exercise is to be split between different sessions, particularly when they are on different days, it may help to make an audio or, when possible, a video recording. At the start of the second session, some or all of the recording can be played back.

3. When seven or eight memories have been shared, ask students to form small groups. Each group should produce a report on whichever aspect(s) of the shared memories they find particularly striking.

4. Completed reports should be circulated from group to group together with a separate comment sheet for each report. After reading the report, each group records a brief comment/evaluation on the comment sheet.

5. Reports are returned to authoring groups. Finally, the tutor reads comments one by one, asking groups to claim the sheet from which the comment is taken if they think it applies to their report. They will know if they were right to claim the sheet – there will not be any comment from their group on it.

COMMENTS

Sometimes we know exactly what a report has to contain when we sit down to write it. At other times we are less sure and wish we had colleagues to advise us and draw our attention to matters we are in danger of overlooking. Many post-graduates who work in research teams will from time to time take their turn at writing up reports. On these occasions it is particularly important to listen carefully to the comments and suggestions of colleagues so that, when written, the report will represent a balanced, consensus view.

Ask students to compare the report writing process practised in this exercise with any they are familiar with in their main subject departments. Would a less formal version of this model be worth adopting as part of the process next time it is their turn to write a report? And more generally, what is the nature of their collaboration with colleagues and are there preferred ways of working as a writing team?

Readership awareness

23   Taking the reader into account

FOCUS

In exercise 24 (*Knowing one's reader*) we try to emphasize the importance of working out who you are writing for. In this exercise, we begin
with a profile of the reader drawn up on an Osgood Semantic Scale. The
writer's task is to take this known reader into account without compro-
mising his or her own integrity. This requires a delicate balancing act
which we observe many of our students are not good at in their regular
writing.

CLASS ORGANIZATION

Grouping: Students first work individually, then in pairs.
Time: 45 minutes.
Materials: Handout (see p. 115.)

THE EXERCISE

1. Distribute a handout to each student, who should complete it for his
   or her own personality and write his or her name in the bottom
   right-hand corner.
2. Collect in the completed handouts, and pair together handouts that
   (at a casual glance) reveal differences in personality.
      Make a list of the pairs. Write the name of the other student in the
   pair on the top left-hand corner of each handout and cut off the names
   from the bottom right-hand corners. Redistribute the handouts to
   those students whose names appear in the top left-hand corners so
   that pairs of students, unknown to each other, have each other's
   scales.
3. Choose an issue for the whole class to write about. A topical issue on
   which students are likely to hold diverse opinions works best. Ask
   each student to write an extended paragraph on the topic which is true
   to his or her feelings and will be acceptable to the person whose
   handout they have just read.
      Alternatively you can ask the students to choose an issue to write
   about while you pair the handouts as described in above.
4. When the writing is completed, pair the relevant students, allow them
   to read what their partners have written, and ask them to discuss how
   they took each other's apparent personalities into account.

COMMENTS

It is impossible to do this exercise without making some clear decisions
about the type of reader one thinks the writing is destined for and taking

WORKSHEET: TAKING THE READER INTO ACCOUNT

MY PERSONALITY

Agnostic								Believer
Deceitful								Honest
Extrovert								Introvert
Feminine								Masculine
Balanced								Paranoid
Intellectual								Physical
Gregarious								Private
Monogamous								Promiscuous
Left								Right
Realistic								Romantic
Open								Secretive
Jocular								Serious
Relaxed								Tense
Feeling								Thinking
Progressive								Traditional

Name ....

this into account at both composing and rewriting stages. With these thoughts in mind, we suggest three follow-up activities:

1. Can students make a profile of each reader for whom they write — tutor, supervisor, examiner, external examiner, conference delegate? To what extent do they think their writing could be improved by thinking more carefully about their readership?

2. Ask students to choose a piece of academic writing in their own field and, as they read it, pause from time to time and draw up a profile of the type of reader the writer appears to be imagining. Do they want to write for the same reader? If for a different reader, how will this be reflected in their writing?
3. In the social sciences in particular the writer's attitudes – political, religious, social – are often important. Ask students in these disciplines to take two pieces of writing on the same topic by different authors and compare them, noting the differences in attitudes of the two authors as well as observable differences in their likely readership. Students may also compare two pieces of writing by the same author but aimed at different readerships and note any resulting differences.

24   Knowing one's reader

FOCUS

When a learner is struggling with a second language, it is only too easy to forget to adapt writing to a particular readership. This skill is crucial in a number of academic writing tasks, such as the assignment, dissertation or thesis – where the nature of the readership is not always immediately clear to the writer. There are also certain other situations outside the classroom where readership awareness is both important and perhaps easier to define. One of these is applying for a job.

The exercise that follows suggests ways of making the writer more aware of his or her readership, although it does not involve an actual writing task.

CLASS ORGANIZATION

Grouping: Students work in pairs initially; then pairs come together to make groups of four.
Time: 40 minutes.
Materials: None.

THE EXERCISE

1. Group the students in fours, and then split each group into two pairs (pair A and pair B) for the first part of the exercise.
   – Pair A's function is to draw up together a list of qualities and experience needed for a particular job. The job is chosen by them, but it should be one that a member of the class might reasonably apply for in an English speaking country.
   – Pair B's function is to list together the general job-relevant achievements, qualities and interests of one member of the pair.
2. Bring the two pairs together and compare the two lists, seeing how the

applicant can reasonably set out their qualities and achievements to match the expectations of the employer. What should be omitted and what will need to be expanded?

COMMENTS

As a follow-up task suggest students each focus on some specific type of writing that is or will be expected from them, such as the methodology chapter of their thesis or a short paper for a post-graduate support group.

They should list everything that the reader will expect to find in it. Next they should list what they are able to supply. How will any deficiencies be covered? What will need to be expanded? In how standard a way will they write the required text? Is this conscious way of thinking about what is expected by the reader a process they should always employ when they write?

25   Selection, prominence and ordering

FOCUS

In exercise 8 (*Ordering material*), we consider ordering from the writer's perspective. Equally, if not more important, is an awareness of reader's perspective – to what extent will different items need to be made prominent for different readers?

This exercise therefore concentrates on how awareness of readership influences the selection of material and the relative prominence the writer gives to different items.

CLASS ORGANIZATION

This exercise may seem more complicated to organize than it actually is.

Grouping: The class works in groups of three or four.

Time: This depends on how long the first part of the exercise (choosing a city) takes and on the work method of the groups – if you aim at 75 minutes, you will need to keep checking that the groups are working to schedule.

Materials: Each group should be given magazine pictures of a distinct type of person, for example: group 1, old people; group 2, children; group 3, young people; group 4, family groups; group 5, the royal family; group 6, film stars and group 7, businessmen and/or business-women. Each group will need enough pictures of their 'type' to be able to distribute one to each of the other groups, so you will need several pictures for each group. Note that the pictures of children, for example, do not need to be of the same child – it is enough for each picture to be recognizable as a child.

117

THE EXERCISE

1. Working as individuals students make short notes, no more than headings, about a city in their own country that they know well. Ask the students to form groups of three or four. The rest of the group asks each person in turn about his or her city, and the questions asked provide further sub-headings.
2. The group should now decide which single city of the three or four described they are going to concentrate on. Having chosen their city, the whole group should try to find out and list as much additional information about it as possible. It often helps to compare it with where everyone is living at present.
3. Distribute the pictures of individuals. Give each group as many pictures as there are other groups in the class.
4. Each group then gives one of its pictures to each of the other groups, and asks for a paragraph explaining why the person in the picture would enjoy living in their city. Thus each group will have to produce a number of different paragraphs aimed at selling their city to different audiences – this will involve careful selection and ordering of information for each target reader.

   Where numbers allow, a good work method is to allocate each person in the group one target reader (e.g., the Queen, an old person etc.) to write a first draft for. The whole group then decides whether to accept the draft as it stands or to make alterations. Take care to explain clearly that groups are not writing a letter to the Queen or an old person: rather, they should describe those features of their city they would wish to draw to the Queen's or an old person's attention.
5. Once the paragraphs are written, they should be passed to the groups supplying the pictures, who will then choose where their person is to live.

COMMENTS

1. If you have tried this exercise successfully on one occasion, the next time you use it you may like to try a grouping technique which is a bit more troublesome to set up but which ensures that each student writes an equal amount. Make sure that there is one fewer person in each group than the total number of groups (i.e., if there are four groups, three people in each; if there are five groups, four people in each, etc.). This will mean that each group member has an individual writing task.
2. This exercise provides a natural way into a discussion of the different formulas preferred by different readers. For example, in some subject areas, the style sheets of British and American journals vary markedly in their attitudes to referencing, abstracting, use of foot- and end-notes, etc. Are students sufficiently aware in their own writing of the

need to present the same information in different ways to different readerships? What opportunities for practising these selection, prominence and ordering skills can they seek out: perhaps twenty minutes to present a spoken summary of a lengthy conference paper destined to be read slowly and carefully later, or the opportunity to talk through in a post-graduate support group a chapter of their thesis which will subsequently be read critically by a team of examiners? In their role as readers, have they come across the same information presented in different ways, e.g., as a paper and as a thesis?

E

Techniques

Expressing complex ideas

26 Relating one's own findings to primary texts

FOCUS

Because so much serious writing relates to writing that has gone before, it is especially important for learners to master relating their own views, findings and arguments to earlier work. For this reason, we suggest a number of exercises in this area. The exercise which follows has as its aims practising relating to a primary text (which is produced as a homework activity), and, optionally, practising relating both to a primary text and to a text that comments on it.

CLASS ORGANIZATION

Grouping: Students work individually or in pairs.
Time: Ten minutes at the end of one class to set up the initial homework, followed by 45 minutes of class time.
Materials: Student homework.

THE EXERCISE

For homework each learner should list on paper ten expectations they had in some area before they actually experienced what they were anticipating. Suitable areas include giving birth, becoming a parent, getting married, living abroad, meeting someone famous, earning one's first pay cheque, going to hospital, owning a car, or moving away from home. Each learner should choose their own area, list the ten expectations for homework and bring them to class for the next session.

In class allow each student to choose whether to work alone or in a pair, but if you choose to follow the optional step 3 of this exercise, students should work individually.

1. Collect the homework and redistribute it so that each student/pair gets someone else's list of expectations in an area that they have experienced themselves. Writing the areas on the blackboard and asking students/pairs to choose one works well. If students arrive without homework, you will need to photocopy some of the completed lists so that there are enough for every student/pair to get one.

2. Each student/pair writes a paragraph comparing their own experiences with the expectations of the original writer. They should be encouraged to treat the original text as the standard of comparison to which their experiences are related.
3. If your students have been working individually, you now have the option of returning the ten item list and the paragraph to the students who produced the lists in the first place. They can then write a second paragraph relating their experiences to their expectations and to the experiences of the paragraph writers.

COMMENTS

We suggest three ways of extending what has been learnt in this exercise into the students' specialist work:
1. Ask students to identify the primary authorities to which their findings or views need to be related in the piece of writing they are working on currently. What balance of prominence should be given to the primary text and to their own findings or views? Is the balance appropriate to the kind of writing they are engaged in (e.g., summary, essay, thesis, chapter, article, etc.)? How might it be different for a different writing task?
2. Ask students to study those parts of an article that relate it to an authority. What linguistic strategies are used when the writer wants:
   – to use the authority to support his or her position?
   – to question the received position?
   – to modify the received position?
3. How important is it to work with authorities, and what sort of attitudes to authorities are usual in the students' disciplines?

27 Comparison – similarity and difference

FOCUS

When considering how to compare one thing with another, there are three points to be made:
– Any two objects or experiences may be similar, dissimilar or identical. And there will of course be degrees of similarity and dissimilarity.
– There is an immensely rich choice of language in this area ranging from straightforward comparative adjective forms, through comparing sentences using conjunctions such as 'whereas', 'whilst', 'although' to 'not only ... but also ...', 'on the one hand ... on the other ...', etc. The writer will then need to select from this range with care.
– Many second or foreign language writers fail to make the comparisons expected in serious writing. This will sometimes be because they do not have sufficient language; but very often it is not the lack of language but the wide range of it that scares language learners off.

This exercise aims to provide students with a considerable body of data obtained from two different sources. Elements of the data will inevitably be similar and dissimilar in varying degrees. And therefore the students will need to struggle to find a range of ways of writing about these similarities and differences.

CLASS ORGANIZATION

Grouping: After filling in an initial questionnaire individually, students should work in pairs for the remainder of the exercise.
Time: 60 minutes.
Materials: Questionnaire (see p. 123).

THE EXERCISE

1. Distribute the questionnaires, which are to be completed individually.
2. Pair students, who then compare their questionnaires and jointly write a substantial paragraph reflecting the degree of similarity and dissimilarity between their two experiences.
3. It is a good idea to ask students to underline all the comparing language in their paragraphs and then to display them on the wall. Encourage the class to compile a vocabulary guide from the paragraphs displayed.

COMMENTS

As this exercise shows, even when we compare superficially similar situations, much of the language we need is used to establish distinctions. It is just these neat distinctions that are very often important in carefully controlled research or in the accurate description and discussion of comparable texts. Below we suggest four ways in which students can be encouraged to think more deeply about this area.

1. Can the students each think of two superficially similar situations they are familiar with from their own reading or research? What are the essential distinctions between these two situations?
2. Ask the students to look for a comparison of superficially similar situations in their specialist literature – what linguistic forms are used to establish the similarities and differences?
3. Ask the students to review essay titles / exam questions in their subject departments to see how often they invite comparisons: what does this say about the value their subject departments place on this activity?
4. If subject departments provide advice in this area of writing, how does it compare with the principles that have emerged while discussing this exercise?

WORKSHEET: COMPARISON — SIMILARITY AND DIFFERENCE

QUESTIONNAIRE: MY LAST EATING EXPERIENCE

1. I drank

2. I ate

3. How many courses did the meal consist of?

4. Were they hot or cold?

5. Precisely what ingredients did the meal contain?

6. Precisely how was it cooked?

7. When did you start it?

8. How long did it take to eat?

9. Which parts were good/enjoyable?
   Which parts were not?

10. Where did the experience occur?

11. Who else was present?

12. Other notable details?

28   Correspondence and non-correspondence

FOCUS

This topic is closely related to the previous exercise on comparison. But in writing about similarity and difference, we were comparing two sets of data of equal standing. In considering correspondence and non-correspondence, we are particularly interested in a data set that does not correspond to an expected norm and in how this fact is conveyed in writing. One obvious example of non-correspondence is the election result that does not fulfil the predictions of the opinion polls, or the particular constituency whose result goes against the general trend.

In this exercise, the expected norm is written in the students' first languages. This is to reinforce the lesson's aim, that of describing the degree of deviation and coincidence of the secondary data set, in this case a piece of writing in English.

CLASS ORGANIZATION

This is an unusual activity in that it is designed as two separate homework exercises. It only works for classes with mixed first languages.

THE EXERCISE

The exercise is done in three stages:
1. Preparation: You need to prepare for this exercise by asking each student to bring a cutting from a first language newspaper to class. The cutting should contain clues as to its contents, for example, a photograph, the name of a well-known person or words that are internationally recognizable. The headline should be translated into English.
2. Assignment A: Students should exchange newspaper cuttings so that each student ends up with a newspaper item in an unfamiliar language. Ask each student to write an article in English which he or she supposes to be as close to the original as possible. This should be done as a homework assignment and brought to class on a particular day.

    Note: Many students have a natural tendency in this situation to approach the supplier of the cutting and ask for help. It is best to pre-empt this by saying that the only help allowable is for the supplier of the cutting to read the article aloud in their first language. This can actually be helpful – occasionally!
3. Assignment B: The original cutting and the English language story should be handed to the student whose newspaper provided the cutting. Ask him or her to write a short analysis detailing the extent to which the English language version corresponds or fails to correspond to the original. This should also be done as a homework assignment.

COMMENTS

1. A possible follow-up in class involves story writers and correspondence checkers working together, uncovering the non-correspondences and commenting on each other's writing. Alternatively, there can be a small group discussion as to the best way of describing the non-correspondences.

   It is also useful to ask students to supply English language translations for possible future use.

2. We suggest a number of questions that it is often helpful to raise with students. Specifically, for what main subject work is the noting of non-correspondence between two texts, historical events, sets of results or other phenomena required? What sort of writing is used for this purpose and how comparable is this to the form of the 'short analysis' written in this exercise?

   To what extent is the noting of non-correspondence required for results obtained or for discussions or articles that originate from two different sources, even, as here, two different cultures? To what extent can or should the noting of such non-correspondences be purely empirical or objective and to what extent and at what stage is evaluation allowable or appropriate?

29 Towards the language of proportion

FOCUS

We rarely give it much thought, but if we did, most of us would be surprised at the variety of ways and the range of vocabulary available for describing what we have here called 'proportion'.

For the intermediate or more advanced language learner, much of this language is probably already part of his or her passive knowledge; even where this is not the case, understanding does not usually present many problems. But when it comes to active production, this is one of those areas in which very few learners express themselves as a native speaker would. For this reason, we have built a first draft and a very deliberate improvement and rewrite phase into this exercise.

The follow-up phase typically reveals something of the range and variety of idiom available in this area.

CLASS ORGANIZATION

Grouping: Students should sit in circles with at least eleven in each one.
Time: 45 minutes.
Materials: One chart (see p. 128) and a half sheet of paper per student.

Part 2   The exercises

THE EXERCISE

1. Students each take a blank chart and write in at the top their own particular hobby or interest. In the first space on the left-hand side they write their name and cross each of the ten boxes to indicate that they are extremely enthusiastic about this hobby. At this stage, each handout will therefore look like this:

CHESS										
Behrang	X	X	X	X	X	X	X	X	X	X

2. Each handout is passed one place round the circle. Each student then writes their name in the next empty space on the left-hand side and puts as many crosses (on a 0–10 scale) as indicates their level of enthusiasm for the activity.

   This step is repeated until the handout is completed, by which time it will look something like this specimen:

COOKING										
Isabella	X	X	X	X	X	X	X	X	X	X
Araceli	X									
Anabel	X	X	X	X	X	X	X			
Gerhardt	X									
Greta	X	X								
Hans Peter	X	X	X	X	X	X	X			
Evi	X									
Tadashi										
Bong Soon	X	X	X	X						
Dakis	X	X	X							

126

3. The last student to write their name on the chart then writes down on a separate piece of paper a single sentence in which the language of proportion and contrast is used to capture as much of the information on the completed chart as possible.

   By way of an example, this is what was written in relation to the chart opposite: 'Apart from Isabella, who is frankly interested in cooking, and two more people who are interested to some extent, the rest of us care little about the subject, or even nothing.'
4. The sentences are then displayed on the wall and the charts returned to the students who started them off.

There are two suggested continuations from here:

5. Each student then writes their own sentence along the lines indicated in 3 above for their own chart.
6. Each student then matches their chart with the appropriate sentence on the wall, and together with their neighbour, attempts to produce a composite sentence bringing together the best qualities of each of the two suggested sentences.

Or alternatively:

5. Each student then matches their chart with the appropriate sentence on the wall and adds a comment to the bottom of the paper on which the sentence is written. The comment should draw attention to whatever aspect(s) of the chart are not properly taken into account in the sentence.
6. The chart and the sentence are then passed to another member of the class, who tries to reformulate the sentence so that it takes this additional data into account.

COMMENTS

1. A useful follow-up activity is to put all the sentences back on the wall and allow the class time to go round making a vocabulary list containing all the language of proportion they can identify in the sentences. This is important because the sentences are usually so easy to understand that the students overlook the need to be aware of as many different ways of expressing these notions as will be revealed.
2. A more sophisticated version of this exercise starts out with a handout that allows negative as well as positive values for each topic.
3. Many students will be working in their subject departments with statistical tables that they need to describe and interpret in natural language. Similarly, studies conducted in one field may yield different findings from studies conducted in related fields, and again these relationships will need to be described and interpreted.
4. The following supplementary activities are suggested:
   – Ask students to study texts in their own disciplines – in what

contexts is the language of proportion found? Can they find particular examples? Texts which represent proportion both in tables/diagrams and by written descriptions are particularly helpful.

— Looking over their last assignments, are there places where their use of the language of proportion could have been more exact or included more of the data it was attempting to describe?

— As a result of doing this exercise, can they produce a list of words and phrases whose meanings may not be completely agreed on by fellow students, e.g., some, a majority, etc.?

— What strategies will they adopt in the future for improving their skills in this language area?

WORKSHEET: TOWARDS THE LANGUAGE OF PROPORTION

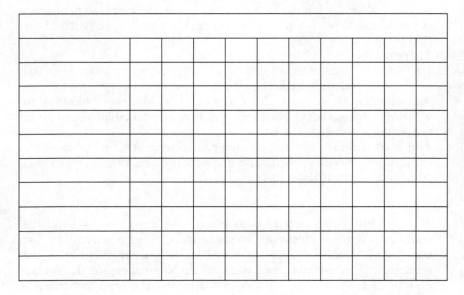

Exactness

30   *Proportion, contrast and expressing an exact meaning*

FOCUS

In this exercise, students first establish a meaning which they set down in writing and then are required to defend the means by which it is expressed. Fellow students, meanwhile, are exploring more exact ways of expressing this meaning and trying to persuade the original writer to make any necessary amendments. The written outcome is only a single sentence, but a sentence which illustrates a very wide range of possibilities for expressing meanings.

A description of this exercise working in the classroom can be found on pp. 48–9.

CLASS ORGANIZATION

Grouping: Students work in groups of between six and ten.
Time: Minimum of 60 minutes.
Materials: One questionnaire per student (see below).

WORKSHEET: PROPORTION, CONTRAST AND EXPRESSING AN EXACT MEANING

	Yes	No	%
1. Would you tell a lie			
2. Do you agree that religious belief			
3. Is marriage			
4. Given absolute freedom to do as you wished, would you			
5. Would you keep quiet if			
6. Do you think is funny?			

THE EXERCISE

1. Ask each group to form a circle. Distribute a questionnaire to each student who should then use the prompts to make up full questions in the spaces provided. The purpose is to try to write questions that are far from easy to answer, for example, 'Would you tell a lie to avoid causing a friend disappointment?'

2. When the questionnaires are completed, each one is passed one place round the circle.

   Without conversing with the question-setter each student now completes the questionnaire in front of them. First, they tick under either 'Yes' or 'No' for each question; and then decide what proportion of the general public would agree with each of their answers, and write that figure in the percentage column. For example:

	Yes	No	%
1. Would you tell a lie *to avoid causing a friend disappointment?*		√	60

3. Each student then chooses any one of the six questions they have answered, and forms a single sentence hypothesis based on the question and the answer to it. You may want to point out that this will require the use of the language of proportion and contrast as the students struggle to relate the question, their response, and the general view. For example, 'Like me, slightly more people would be unwilling to tell a lie to avoid causing a friend disappointment than would tell the lie.'

4. A volunteer then shares their hypothesis with the rest of the group, who should be encouraged to comment/request elucidation/suggest alterations, etc. The discussion continues until everyone is satisfied that the hypothesis relates all the data (i.e., the question, the yes or no answer and the general viewpoint) as exactly as is possible in one sentence.

   It is not always possible for a group to reach a satisfactory outcome. They should be allowed to ask their colleague to go away and try to take on board as much of the discussion as possible in a rewritten version to be brought into class the next day.

   If time allows, the process can be repeated with another hypothesis.

COMMENTS

There are several ways in which this exercise can be followed up:
1. Ask students to bring to class two complex sentences of this variety, one from their own writing and the other from a textbook or article. In what ways could the intended meaning be more exactly expressed? What objections could be raised to the original form?
2. As a result of having had to defend the essential meaning of their sentence in this exercise, what have students learnt about handling the suggestions/criticisms of others? To what extent were they too defensive, insufficiently open or not forceful enough in talking about their ideas and the way they were expressed in past discussions of their writing with tutors or supervisors?

3. Ask students to choose a complex sentence in a textbook each day for a week and consider exactly what it means, in terms of both what it states and what it implies, and why the reader decides this is what it means.
4. Are there ways of improving their rereading skills to which this exercise draws attention?

31 *Revealing attitudes*

FOCUS

When we write, it is very important to learn how to express our own views in a way that persuades rather than alienates the reader. In the exercise that follows, students are often surprised at the very wide range of more and less sophisticated ways of expressing an opinion that emerge. There is much to be learnt from this exercise about preferred ways of revealing our own attitudes and about precisely how to do it.

CLASS ORGANIZATION

Grouping: Initially students work individually or in pairs; subsequently in groups of four or five.
Time: At least 75 minutes – more if you use television or radio recordings. If it helps, this exercise can easily be split between two sessions.
Materials: News items, coloured card and (optionally) felt pens for writing on card.

THE EXERCISE

1. Choose a topic of contemporary news interest about which more or less everyone may be expected to have an opinion. An international political question, such as apartheid or terrorism, or a domestic social issue would be ideal.
   Choose four or five short news items or comments, each focusing on a different aspect of the issue. Ideally, if the facilities allow, two/three newspapers, one television broadcast on video and one radio extract give variety, although four or five brief newspaper items are fine.
2. Supply lots of small pieces of card in three different colours and establish that each colour relates to a reaction: favourable, unfavourable or mixed. Individual students or pairs of students study each of the items in turn. (If you use audio or video recordings, it works well to leave the cassette player or VCR and monitor on open access. Programme automatic rewind if your equipment has this facility; otherwise, clearly indicate start and finish points.)
   As they study each item, the students should decide whether their

attitude is favourable, unfavourable or mixed. They can then take a
piece of colour coded card for each item and write a short response in
which they reveal their attitude. For example, 'The attitude of the US
President to the affairs of a country thousands of miles away is
difficult to support.' These responses should be pinned to the wall
alongside the appropriate item.
3. When stage 2 is completed, the class divides into as many groups as
there are items (i.e., four or five groups). Each group is allocated to
one item and is responsible for grading the responses to it according to
their degree of sophistication/persuasiveness.

It is, on the whole, best to grade each of the original categories
(favourable, unfavourable, mixed) separately – though this partly
depends on how many there are in each category.

The responses are then put back on the wall with the most
persuasive at the top and the most alienating at the bottom.
4. Finally, allow students time to circulate freely trying to identify
precisely what features of each response reveal the writer's attitude. It
helps to invite the students to underline what they identify and/or
make notes.

COMMENTS

In order to sharpen your students' awareness in the area practised in this
exercise, you could ask them to discuss each of the following statements:
– The extent to which the attitude of the writer is relevant varies
according to the academic discipline involved.
– Tutors/supervisors prefer students to be more critical in their writing.
– Negative or critical attitudes should usually be implied by the choice of
words rather than stated directly.
– Expressing positive attitudes reflects well on the writer.
– The rules for overseas students (outsiders) are different from the rules
for native speakers (insiders).
Three strategies that students often find useful:
– Ask their tutor/supervisor to draw their attention to an opportunity to
reveal an attitude that the student failed to take in the last writing
assignment.
– When they next find themselves writing an attitude revealing sentence,
spend ten minutes thinking of two other ways of revealing the attitude
and then decide which of the three versions is most appropriate.
– Ask a fellow student if they may read one of their assignments in order
to identify successful and less successful ways in which attitudes are
revealed.

32 Describing spatial relations

FOCUS

In many kinds of writing in a work context, we are required to describe how a system is set up within a spatial framework. It is notoriously difficult to describe an interrelated layout accurately. It is also extremely difficult to judge how successful we have been in our description. This exercise provides an opportunity both to describe a spatial layout and to find out how successful the description is.

CLASS ORGANIZATION

Grouping: Groups of six.
Time: Minimum of 60 minutes – the time varies considerably with the level of the class.
Materials: Each group will need a sheet of A4 paper and six shapes: a triangle, a circle and a square cut out of card of one colour, and a second triangle, circle and rectangle of different sizes cut out of card of another colour. It should be very nearly but not quite possible to assemble the six shapes on the sheet of A4 in such a way that no part of any of them overlaps the sheet of paper. For example, the six shapes will nearly fit within the scaled down A4 outline below:

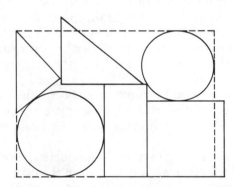

If you have groups of five, use only five shapes and cut the sheet of A4 down proportionately. It is crucial that each group has shapes of different sizes from the other groups but it is relatively quick and easy to make sets of shapes if you start with two pieces of different coloured card that together are slightly bigger than the sheet of A4. Do not waste time measuring the shapes or making sure that the circles are perfect – just cut them out quickly. If they fit within the sheet of A4, you can always cut it down slightly afterwards.

THE EXERCISE

1. Distribute a sheet of A4 and six shapes to each group. Ask the students to arrange the shapes on the sheet so that as little as possible of any shape extends beyond the edge of it.
2. The group now writes on each shape a description of its location. This description may refer to colour, shape, size, placement on sheet of A4, and relation to other shapes. The purpose is to write as economical a description as conveys the location of the shapes exactly.
3. When the description is written, each group makes a simple copy of it, removes its shapes from the sheet of A4 and passes them to another group, which attempts to reassemble them in accordance with the descriptions.

   Once a group thinks it has the solution, it sends for the original group to check, and together the two groups discuss any possible ways of making the descriptions more explicit.

COMMENTS

1. The shapes can be reused in another class if you paste paper over the side the students have written on.
2. We present this exercise in its simplest form. More person related variations on the theme are easy to invent. For example, with groups of eight to twelve, each member of the group draws their house and the group then arranges the houses, as though in a street, in the most aesthetically satisfying order. Descriptions of the relative locations of the houses are then written on the back of each one and the exercise continues as in 3 above.
3. This exercise draws attention both to the difficulties of writing exactly and economically and also to the problems inadequate descriptions cause for the reader. The following suggestions help to reinforce these points:
   - Ask students to exchange recently completed pieces of writing and explain to each other what is unclear in the other's writing.
   - Does any member of the class face a specific writing task comparable to the one posed by this exercise? Will the class agree to spend a session trying to solve their fellow student's problem collectively?
   - Are there other kinds of writing task which are helped by bearing in mind the principles established in this exercise?

33 *Using technical terms – and making their meanings clear*

FOCUS

The aim of this exercise is to confront students with this problem: they need to use a technical term, and they know precisely what process or phenomenon it refers to – how then should they choose between the kinds of strategy for explaining it discussed below?

In any subject area where knowledge has expanded rapidly, there will inevitably be a set of technical and semi-technical terms to describe this knowledge. Sometimes, as in the case of computer terminology, these technical terms pass into common usage. But in most cases, such terms are understood only by a small group of insiders. For that reason, those who use such terms often need to explain them to their readers. How is this done?

Sometimes a writer chooses to describe a process first, and then adds, '... this process is sometimes/frequently/commonly known as / referred to as resonance'. (To illustrate possible techniques we will use the term 'resonance' as you will notice.) Alternatively, he or she may write, 'Resonance, or the condition in which a surface or space enters into vibration in response to sound waves...' Here, what follows the use of 'or' is an explanation of the preceding technical term, 'resonance'. Or, if we are unsure whether our readers understand the term, we may write, 'If we take / Taking resonance to refer to the condition in which a surface...'

Of course, it is not always so simple – there are bound to be times when the same apparently technical term is used differently by different experts. We may wish to reflect this fact in the way we gloss or explain it. For example, 'Whilst Smith used resonance to mean..., more recently physicists have typically expanded this definition to include...'

And we should not forget that these four strategies:
– describing a process/phenomenon/object, etc., and then naming it;
– technical term + 'or' + explanation;
– taking technical term x to mean...;
– offering two or more explanations of a single technical term;
are by no means an exhaustive list of the ways a writer has of making clear the meanings of technical terms.

CLASS ORGANIZATION

Grouping: Groups of four students are best but the exercise will work
  with groups of three.
Time: 60 minutes.
Materials: Copies of the Focus section of this exercise, from the beginning of the second paragraph to the end.

135

F

THE EXERCISE

1. Ask students to work in groups of three or four. Give each group of students a different question to consider. Suitable topics include:
   - What has been happening to your English since you left school / since you came to Britain / over the last year?
   - How has your personality changed in the last five years?
   - How have the relations between the superpowers altered over the last five years?
   - What physical changes do you see in yourself since the age of (supply suitable age)?
   - Can you relate political changes to economic changes in the recent history of your country?
   - What major phases can you trace in the relationship between yourself and your parents/children/neighbour?

   It often works well to put the possible topics on the blackboard — preferably dotted about at random and circled — and let each group choose which they will work on. Remember to make sure that each group chooses a different topic.

   Once each group has its topic, encourage them to talk their topics through carefully and make notes of the major points that arise. It often helps in making the notes to record in one column those experiences that are common throughout the group, and in another those that are particular to an individual.

2. Once each group has a clear understanding of the process or phenomenon they have been discussing, instruct them to invent a technical term to describe it. It does not matter what this term is, so long as it is original and complex. If by a happy coincidence there is a word for this phenomenon in the language of a group member, this non-English term can be used. Alternatively, a compound noun containing elements from two or three of the languages of the group works well.

3. Give each group a copy of the extract from the Focus section of this exercise. Each member of the group chooses a different one of the four strategies to make the meaning of the group's technical term clear. This should be done individually in writing.

4. Once each group has written the explanations, they can be passed from group to group for comment/discussion, or read aloud and discussed.

COMMENTS

The extent to which a technical term needs to be glossed depends on the readership. Can students illustrate this with examples from their own subject areas? Which glossing strategy would they choose for each of the

136

examples and why? What other glossing strategies have they found? What other glossing strategies are useful?

Ask students to look for examples of technical terms being redefined in the literature of their subject areas. How is this done?

34 Being precise about time

FOCUS

When they locate events in a time frame, our learners very often do not use the full range of options available in English. This exercise highlights some of those options and is also about the extent to which it is (a) feasible, and (b) sensible to expand sentences and make them more accurate.

This exercise may be used before exercise 35 (*Using English verbs*).

CLASS ORGANIZATION

Grouping: Students should work in a circle.
Time: 60 minutes.
Materials: One copy of sheet A (see p. 138) and one blank sheet (to be called sheet B) per student.

THE EXERCISE

1. Each student lists the names of ten former teachers, together with the subjects they taught, and the year(s) in which they were their teachers on sheet A. Next, each student writes down one sentence that each teacher would say about them. Finally, on a separate sheet, B, each student writes a one sentence general report for themselves based on the information on sheet A.

   In the next two stages sheet A is going to be passed round the circle while sheet B stays with the writer.

2. Sheet A is passed one place round the circle. Each student now writes a one sentence report based on the information on the sheet A currently in front of them. This report should be written on the back of sheet A.

   When this is done, sheet A is passed one place further round the circle.

3. For the next twenty minutes to half hour, each student will expand the sentence on the sheet A in front of him or her as instructed by the teacher. After each expansion, the sheet should be passed one further place round the circle. The teacher's instructions to the students are:
   Incorporate:
   — 'be' + 'ing' (present or past as appropriate)
   — 'have' + 'en' (present or past as appropriate)

Part 2   The exercises

WORKSHEET: BEING PRECISE ABOUT TIME

SHEET A

Teacher	Subject	Year(s)	Comment

- point of time (adverb or adverb phrase)
- frequency (adverb or adverb phrase)
- duration (adverb or adverb phrase)
- clause beginning with 'when'/'whenever'/'before'/'after'
- modal auxiliary (can/could, may/might, etc.).

As you go through the list, you will probably find some people are consistently quicker than others. If necessary, write the instructions up on the board when the relative speeds start to get problematical.

Sentences should not be expanded when it cannot be done consistently with the information given on the sheet.

To illustrate what will happen, imagine the report I receive says, 'John does not work as hard as he could, and sometimes his behaviour lets him down.' The instruction is to incorporate 'be'+'ing'. Clearly I can add this to the first part of the sentence but not to the second, so I rewrite the report accordingly, 'John is not working as hard as he could, and sometimes his behaviour lets him down.' I then pass it round the circle to my neighbour, who is instructed to incorporate 'have'+'en' to the sentence as it now stands, to give, 'John has not been working as hard as he could, and sometimes his behaviour has let him down.'

4. When the expansions are complete, the sheets should be returned to their original owners who may now compare them with their original report on sheet B.

COMMENTS

For students at this level it is not the forms that are problematical but their functions. In addition, the overuse of what is feasible or grammatically possible is likely to result in sentences that are too elaborate – as the exercise demonstrates. How then are students to judge the right balance between naively simple and over elaborate verb phrase constructions? This partly depends on the extent to which students recognize that verb form decisions and temporal adverbials are interdependent.

Ask students to spend some time searching out sentences in their own specialist literature that contain a combination of two or more of the seven features practised in the exercise. What sorts of combinations are favoured?

Ask students to review their last piece of writing. Are there places where the time adverbials and verb phrase forms could more precisely capture temporal concepts?

Acknowledgement: We first came across the idea of wondering what our teachers would say about us now at a Pilgrims seminar.

35   Using English verbs

FOCUS

At the level these exercises are aimed at, student problems with the use of English verbs are not usually morphological (i.e., form related). More often, a student fails to match a form with its context. The context can be linguistic (e.g., 'since I started to work in London') or non-linguistic (e.g., a student needs to find the right way of explaining that the action was ongoing right up to yesterday).

This exercise therefore aims to practise the use of sophisticated verb forms in appropriate linguistic and real world contexts. In it two types of sentence will not be 'rewarded' – by which we mean written either on the board or a wall chart:

– those whose verbs are formally correct and appear in appropriate contexts but which fail to describe the world as it is (or, in this exercise, as it was);
– those whose verbs either are not formally correct and/or do not appear in appropriate contexts.

For a sentence to be 'rewarded' in this exercise, three things are necessary:

– the verb forms must be correct;
– the verb's linguistic context must be appropriate, e.g., 'yesterday' only with past;
– the sentence must describe the world truthfully.

This may sound a bit complicated, but as you become involved in the exercise, you will see what it all amounts to – and, we hope, why we have done it this way.

CLASS ORGANIZATION

Grouping: This works best with small classes of up to fifteen students, but will work with classes of various sizes if you make the necessary organizational adjustments.

Time: Up to 75 minutes.

Materials: Large sheets of card (optional).

THE EXERCISE

1. Ask each student to think of a personal belonging of special significance to them. It can be something they own now or a childhood belonging – unusual possessions are quite acceptable. The students should write the name of their belonging (e.g., watch, scarf, bicycle) on the board.
2. You need to reduce the number of belongings on the board to one for every five students. So if you have fifteen in the class, you are going to ask the students to select the three belongings they are most interested

in learning more about. Remove the others from the board, and write the names of the three owners beside the three remaining belongings.

Ask the students to 'specialize' in just one of the three belongings in such a way that five students are specializing in each of the three belongings. (No one may specialize in their own belonging.)

3. Each student should now write five separate sentences about the belonging they are specializing in and its owner. Their sentences must use any five different verb forms chosen from a selection provided by the teacher. The purpose is to write interesting sentences which turn out to be true. For example, 'Xiao-ling must have ridden her bicycle a lot when she was young because she hates walking so much.'

We suggest you offer students the choice of five of the following forms:

past	past progressive
present perfect	past perfect
present perfect progressive	past perfect progressive
used to	might have
must have	could have

It is important to offer a choice of forms, which can be illustrated with examples if necessary, so that the writers can concentrate on trying to write what will turn out to be true sentences. Thus students will not be 'rewarded' for writing about Xiao-ling and her bicycle if what they write turns out to be untrue or inaccurate.

4. When the writing is over, you will have a large number of sentences to be read aloud. So you will need a criterion for which ones are actually to be read, for example, those relating to object A, those featuring form B or sentences students want to offer because they are especially confident of their truth. To be written on the board or on a wallchart, a sentence must get past both the teacher, who filters out ungrammatical sentences, and the student whose belonging is being written about, who must confirm that the sentence is indeed true.

COMMENTS

Two possible extension activities are:

— Ask students to take a thousand word passage of academic writing in their subject area and compare it with a thousand words of their own academic writing. How many times do each of the verb forms suggested in the exercise appear in the two extracts? Can they identify places where the verb forms they tend to avoid would have been appropriate in their writing?

— Ask students to photocopy a page of a textbook, white out all the complete verbs, number each space and provide a numbered list of the verb roots. This should be brought to class and exchanged with a fellow student's similarly prepared page. They then write what they think are the correct verb forms in each space.

Writing skills

36 Collocation in the verb phrase

FOCUS

Many school taught learners never seem to progress beyond a certain stage in the development of their productive second language usage. We think that for many learners this is to do with failing to move from a syntactic to a semantic system for constructing sentences. To take an example, learners are either taught, not necessarily as the result of overt or conscious explanation, or teach themselves that there are three parts to a sentence like *The cat sat on the mat* – 'the cat', subject, 'sat', verb and 'on the mat', preposition phrase. And in terms of constituent structure, this is of course correct.

But another way of looking at the same sentence is to note that only a limited number of nouns (or referring words) can be the subject of *sit*; that *mat* is one of a relatively limited set of nouns suitable for this sentence; and that *on* is one of a small set of suitable prepositions to be collocated with *sit*. It is with this kind of collocation that we are concerned in this exercise.

Our argument is that many learners are taught to think too structurally about the language they are learning, and fail to perceive the essential semantic collocations between, for example, verb (or predicate) and preposition. And if you never learn to think in the language in this way, you will never get beyond a certain point. It makes no real sense to think of *I am cross with Jane* as composed of the three constituents 'I', 'am cross' and 'with Jane', when the essential semantic tie is between 'cross' and 'with'.

We have found that awareness raising exercises like this one, together with the kind of follow-up activity recommended, often enable the student who is stuck at the stage we describe above to make a quantum leap. Moreover, the rapid improvement that results is very readily perceived by the learner too.

CLASS ORGANIZATION

Grouping: This is a whole class activity with an individual writing element.
Time: 45 minutes.
Materials: Several very small pieces of paper per student.

THE EXERCISE

1. The class should sit in a circle if possible. Ask the learners to spend two or three minutes thinking of all the moods they have been in over

142

the preceding 24 hours (e.g., cross, bored, amused, proud, etc.). When they have six or eight words each, ask everyone to write their mood words up on the board.

2. In the remaining 30 minutes, each student should write as many one sentence 'letters' to as many colleagues as the time allows. Each 'letter' should take the form of a one sentence personal question using one of the mood words on the board. For example, using the word *proud*:

Dear Mohammed,
Was your father proud of you when you grew your moustache?
                    Your friend,
                        Ali

As well as writing one sentence letters, students should reply to those they receive. If short of time, they should give low priority to replying to letters where the preposition used is 'by'.

COMMENTS

To build on what has been done in class ask your students to spend ten minutes each evening noting every use of a preposition and its preceding predicate (verb or adjective) in a page of the academic text they are reading at the time. These collocations should be listed in the students' vocabulary books. This is particularly valuable not only because it helps to reinforce the importance of semantic links between words; it also helps students to shift their passive knowledge into their active repertoire. For example, everyone in an EAP class at the level we are writing for will understand 'be in sympathy *with*' / 'feel sympathy *for*' / 'be sympathetic *towards*', but how many actually use these expressions, or when they do, use them accurately?

37 Accounting for facts

FOCUS

This exercise focuses on a relation weaker than causality. How can a given fact or set of facts be accounted for? What do we appeal to in order to explain why a particular thing is as it is? And what range of language will assist us?

CLASS ORGANIZATION

Grouping: Students work in fours.
Time: 60 minutes.
Materials: None.

THE EXERCISE

1. Ask students to make lists of their ambitions for their children or if they are not parents, imaginary children. Encourage them to be specific and detailed. Then group students in fours and ask them to share these ambitions.
2. Explain that the purpose of the exercise is to discover why a particular student has the ambitions they do or thinks they are important. Ask for one volunteer in each group who is prepared to have this investigated by the other members of the group.

   A good work method is for the other three students in the group to try the volunteer with various suggestions. And when a measure of agreement is reached in any area, to try for an acceptable written sentence.

   A possible explanation for why a particular ambition is held may be just as useful as an apparently cast-iron one and will require still more skilful framing in a sentence – so if the three students and the volunteer disagree, the three students should still write a sentence. The activity works best if you ensure that all the students in each group, including the volunteer, write each sentence – this makes the next stage much easier.
3. Once six or seven sentences have been written down, the whole group of four should turn its attention to the best way of linking these together to form a persuasive account of why a particular student holds the ambitions he or she does.

FOLLOW-UP

A useful follow-up is for one group to talk through their findings before reading their account aloud. This allows other members of the class to question the way things have been put in writing.

COMMENTS

Academic research frequently operates by collecting the data that will establish statistically provable causal relationships. But sometimes, and especially in less empirically founded methods of inquiry, the relationships asserted are the products of reasoning rather than statistical analysis. This is especially true in the arts and at undergraduate level where essay writing typically requires students to account for phenomena in a non-empirical way.

Ask students to review a piece of writing in their specialist area to identify the various ways in which the writer seeks to establish reasons for his or her beliefs. How important is such argumentation in academic writing? Is writing in an area that relies on a non-empirical method of relating phenomena more difficult than writing in an area that relies on an empirical method?

38 Cohesion

FOCUS

Recent theoretical literature has demonstrated the immense range of cohesive systems in a language. Writers obviously need to be aware of this range and of the particular lexical choices through which cohesion is effected in English.

This exercise draws students' attention to these features of English by inviting them to rewrite or reformulate what has already been written in such a way as to make it cohere with an existing text.

You will need to take account of your group's attitude. The version we suggest is for co-operative groups who want to work slowly and help each other so that everyone can learn as much as possible. But a more competitive group may like more 'dominoes' each and may try to find a 'winner'.

CLASS ORGANIZATION

Grouping: Divide the class into groups of eight to twelve students.
Time: Allow one hour for the exercise plus extra time for a tutor-led discussion of what has emerged.
Materials: Two 'dominoes' per student, i.e., sheets of A5, each divided into two halves by a line drawn down the middle.

THE EXERCISE

1. The class must first agree on a common theme to write about – a country currently in the news, or any controversial topic work well.
   Distribute two 'dominoes' to each student, who should write four sentences on the agreed theme that make sense together, one in each of the spaces on the two 'dominoes':

| Sentence 1 | Sentence 2 | | Sentence 3 | Sentence 4 |

2. Then, play a game of dominoes as follows: invite someone to put a domino on the table. The student to their left can now add a domino to either end of the original one, but it must make some sort of general

sense and the student playing the domino should explain how the two dominoes fit together. Almost certainly they will need to suggest changes or additions to their own writing and/or to the domino on the table in order to justify placing the two together. It is a good thing to encourage general discussion at this stage and to make it clear that the group as a whole is expected to agree that the two dominoes in amended form do indeed go together. If no agreement is reached the player misses a go.

3. Continue playing round the circle until all the dominoes are on the table. Clearly, this exercise tends to get more difficult when each player is reduced to a single domino and when the existing text has become more substantial.

COMMENTS

The following statements provide useful discussion points:
— Because you have to think so hard about how to express each sentence in a second language, it is difficult to keep the preceding sentence in mind, and this is one reason why the two sentences may not always cohere properly.
— A major rereading skill is to check for cohesion and a major rewriting skill is to be able to improve it where required.
— Each sentence should be reread at the time it is written to check for cohesion.

Many students have little conscious awareness of the ways cohesion and coherence are effected in English. Working on both teacher selected texts and their own written assignments often helps to raise consciousness in this area and demonstrate the importance of cohesion in good writing.

Acknowledgement: This exercise is based on an idea for picture dominoes where a face/person and a building/landscape are linked, which we first met through David Hill of the British Institute in Milan.

39   Collocation in the noun phrase

FOCUS

Collocation, or the placing of two or more words together in a phrase, is one of the most difficult areas of English. How is a second or foreign language user to know that *macro-economics* is a recognised term, and yet *macro-politics* not? Or that a *contemporary building* is much more natural than a *contemporary bridge*?

This exercise aims to raise students' consciousness in this area rather than to give them guiding principles. Important things that students need to be conscious of certainly include:
— the notion that serious writing favours this sort of collocation;

– the fact that collocation is often idiomatic, for example, *a good neighbour* isn't a moral person who lives next door;
– the need to recognize collocation.

In order to reinforce these notions, we have introduced an element of competition into this exercise – with points being scored for idiomatic collocations that are recognized by the learner.

CLASS ORGANIZATION

Grouping: Individual preparatory homework; in class students move from one partner to another in rapid succession.
Time: 30–45 minutes depending on class size.
Materials: None.

THE EXERCISE

1. Preparation: This needs to be done by students before coming to class. Each student should think of:
   – a two word specialist term in their own field of interest, for example, *electron microscope, patristic theology, insider dealing*;
   – a two word term to describe a non-specialist or leisure interest, for example, *contemporary design, electoral reform, fast cars.*
   Additionally, each student should attach four modifiers to the second item in the term, so as to bring to class a specialist term and a non-specialist one, each modified by five typical modifiers. For example: *electron microscope + early microscope, compound microscope, solar microscope, laboratory microscope*; *contemporary design + good design, set design, clean design, grand design.*
2. In class: Each student moves from one partner to another in rapid succession. The purpose is to see how many of the ten modifiers their partner has chosen will collocate with each of the two nouns they have chosen. The scoring is as follows:
   Your modifier collocates with your partner's noun – 0 points.
   Your modifier does not collocate with your partner's noun – 1 point.
   Your partner's modifier collocates with your noun – 2 points.
   Your partner's modifier was one of the five in your list – 3 points.
   Encourage students to list successful collocations.

COMMENTS

A useful type of self-made reference material is a small alphabetically organized notebook which includes phrases, and especially collocations, alongside the usual spelling and vocabulary items. This is a good opportunity to get your students started on this sort of notebook if they do not already keep one. Any collocations they enter are best illustrated in a sentence.

It can also be very illuminating to look at actual texts to see just how full of collocation they are. With this in mind we suggest the following consolidation activity:

1. Ask students to compare three pages of a specialist textbook with three pages of their own writing by underlining all the complex noun phrases in each and then deciding what proportion are idiomatic or set collocations in the sense meant in this exercise.
2. How many of the single nouns in their own three pages could be productively collocated with a modifier?
3. Instruct students to keep this sort of collocation in the forefront of their thinking in their next piece of writing.

40   Defining by appeal to form and function

FOCUS

Sometimes we define an object by referring to its form and sometimes by referring to its function. Thus *Webster's Dictionary* first defines the word 'book' in terms of form as 'a formal written document'. Later it offers a functional definition – 'something felt to be a source of enlightenment or instruction'.

Quite often both types of definition are required. This is particularly true in academic contexts where the very existence of phenomena is often explained by the functions which they perform. Thus an academic discussion of rodents would obviously seek to relate the species' formal dental properties to the uses or functions to which rodents put their teeth.

It is very easy, especially in a second language, to overlook the extent to which a combined formal and functional definition adds clarity to one's writing. This exercise aims to practise defining by appeal to form and function: it demonstrates how difficult it can be for a non-specialist to understand the function when only a formal definition is provided; and to imagine the form when only a functional definition is provided.

CLASS ORGANIZATION

Grouping: Individual preparatory homework; in class students work either individually or in pairs.
Time: 40 minutes.
Materials: Exotic objects provided by students.

THE EXERCISE

1. Preparation: Ask each student to find one object which they suspect will be unknown to the majority of their classmates. It may be particular to an individual's work or culture, or it may be something collected from somewhere exotic on a student's travels. The object should be brought to class (but kept hidden in a bag) together with

three sheets of paper. The first sheet contains both a formal and a functional definition of the object, the second only a formal, and the third only a functional – as below:

FORMAL DEF	FORMAL DEF	
mu mu mu mu	*mu mu mu mu*	
mu mu mu mu	*mu mu mu*	
mu mu mu mu	*mu mu mu*	
FUNCTIONAL DEF		FUNCTIONAL DEF
mu mu mu mu		*mu mu mu*
mu mu mu mu		*mu mu mu*
mu mu mu mu		*mu mu mu*

The object should not be referred to by name in any of the definitions.

Because it is so important for everyone to bring homework, you may decide to withdraw any students without homework and give them a separate task.

2. In class:
   – Collect in the sheets that contain both formal and functional definitions and set them aside for the moment.

   The class may work individually or in pairs. Assuming a paired class, each pair will now have four sheets: two with formal and two with functional definitions. First, the two formal definitions should be exchanged for another pair's. Then the two functional definitions should be exchanged for those of a second, different pair.

   – Each pair tries to write functional definitions on the sheets containing formal definitions, and formal definitions on the sheets containing functional.

   While the class is working, cut the first sheets in half and pin them to the wall in random order.

   – When the writing has been completed, ask the pairs to find the correct definitions to complement those they received at the beginning of the session and remove them from the wall. When this has been done, the exotic objects may be revealed.

Remember that it is possible to find the correct definitions just by matching the handwriting. You may decide to allow this, or you may ask for the homework to be done in such a way that the sheet containing both formal and functional definitions is typed or written in two different hands.

COMMENTS

This exercise highlights the problems of understanding what object is being referred to when only a formal or only a functional definition is available. In actual texts it is rarely anything like so problematical since the object is usually named even when the definition is only of its formal or functional properties.

Can students find examples of inadequate definitions in academic texts or in their own work? Are the definitions inadequate because what is defined is unclear or simply because the convention requires both formal and functional definitions and only one is given? Can they remedy those they find in their work?

The sorts of objects that need to be defined will obviously depend on the readership envisaged. Have students correctly judged when to define in a specimen piece of their own writing? If students are talking their research through with colleagues and find themselves defining terms, is this an indication of the need to check that this has been done, and done properly, in their writing?

41   Citing evidence in support of a position

FOCUS

When we write, it is all too easy to make assertions. Much more difficult is the search for the evidence that supports our assertions. In general, the assertions that we make will only prevail if the evidence supports our position. This exercise is largely about recognizing that adequate evidence is needed to support positions that are taken up.

But there is a further difficulty. Sometimes the position we wish to support itself changes, and the evidence that was adequate before does not seem so forceful any more. This exercise recognizes that positions tend to get modified as we rethink and that evidence that was satisfactory before may not be sufficient to support a changed position.

CLASS ORGANIZATION

Grouping: Maximum class size 26.
Time: 60 minutes.
Materials: One copy of the outlined figures for each student (see p. 152), self-adhesive labels (optional), writing paper.

THE EXERCISE

1. Each student should be allocated the number of one of the outlined figures which may be stuck or pinned on them. Eventually students will be working in the following small groups:

   Group A: 13, 14, 15, 16, 17, 23, 24, 25.
   Group B: 7, 8, 9, 10, 11, 21.
   Group C: 12, 18, 19, 20, 22, 26.
   Group D: 1, 2, 3, 4, 5, 6.

   If you have fewer than twenty students, do not allocate the numbers for Group D, fewer than 14, do not allocate the numbers for C and D, etc.

   Next, distribute to each student a copy of the outlined figures. Each learner should then decide, without any discussion with anyone else in the class, what the outline with the same number as themselves is doing (e.g., 11 might be conducting an orchestra, 26 watching from a gallery, etc.). Having decided this, each student writes a short paragraph stating what they are doing and giving as many reasons in support of this position as they can find in the figure.

   Meanwhile the teacher writes the groupings up on the board and, when everyone has written their paragraphs, asks the students to get into groups as indicated.

2. Each student reads their paragraph to the other members of the group. The members of the group must decide, as a result of studying the outline carefully, which of the activities described best fits the group as a whole.

   The groups should write a substantial paragraph citing as much evidence as they can justifying everyone in the group being engaged in the single activity chosen.

3. Finally, each group reveals or mimes their activity to the other groups and reads out their paragraph.

COMMENTS

To apply the lessons of this exercise to the requirements of their academic subject, ask students to review an essay or piece of their own writing that takes up a position. How is the evidence presented and at what stage is the position stated? What different possibilities do the various students' reviews suggest?

Can the students draw any parallels between the way they worked in this exercise and the way they work in their subject departments – for example, when a new position has to be adopted?

WORKSHEET: CITING EVIDENCE IN SUPPORT OF A
POSITION

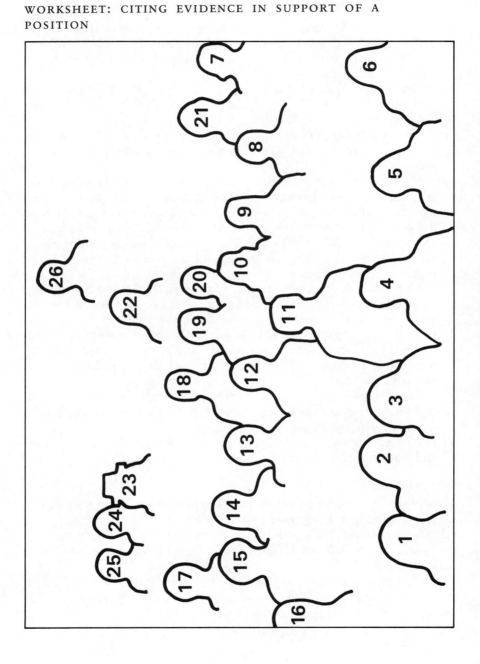

42   Punctuation

FOCUS

Although punctuation is not the be-all and end-all of good writing, most students agree that it does contribute to the value of their writing. The teaching of punctuation mechanically or in isolation may or may not work, depending on the type of student you are teaching. But if you can give students the feeling that good punctuation adds a star quality to good writing, then they are more likely to take it seriously.

So in this activity, students are encouraged to assess the quality of their writing both in terms of its relevance or the extent to which it makes a good point and in terms of how appropriately it is punctuated.

CLASS ORGANIZATION

Grouping: Students work in groups of four or five. It is a good idea to work with the whole class for the last twenty minutes provided there are not more than five groups.

Time: 75 minutes.

Materials: Each member of the class will need four pieces of different coloured card.

THE EXERCISE

1. Group the students and distribute four pieces of different coloured card to each student. Agree a topic with the whole class. Something related to life style is a good choice – health and fitness works particularly well.

   Each student should write four sentences on the chosen theme: on the colour A card, a sentence containing a comma; on the colour B card, a sentence containing a colon; on the colour C card, a sentence containing a semi-colon; on the colour D card, a sentence containing an exclamation mark.

2. Each group then pools its sentences and considers them one colour or punctuation mark at a time. Each set of sentences should be graded twice. The first time they should be graded according to how good a point they make: if there are five sentences, the best scores five points and the worst scores one point. The second time they should be graded according to how effectively the point of punctuation is used – again on a one to five scale if there are five sentences. The grades are then added together, and the sentence with the highest composite score set aside. This process should be repeated with each of the other three sets of sentences.

3. Each group will now have four quality sentences set aside.

   Bring all the groups together to play in the super league. Choose one category (e.g., colon) and write the quality colon sentences from each group up on the board. The whole class then decides which sentence wins the super league.

4. It is useful to display the quality sentences on the wall and to encourage students to note them down.

COMMENTS

At this level of work, punctuation should be as much a matter of judgement as a matter of knowledge. But it is worth checking and filling in any knowledge gaps that may emerge in discussion.

Ask students to take their last written assignment and make up to ten punctuation and related consequential changes in it. They should then team up with a fellow student and together they decide if the changes improve the writing, and if they do, why.

Ask students to compare the punctuation of two writers in their own field. Is there a discernible difference in their punctuation strategies? If so, which is the more skilful punctuator?

The idea that a particular feature is a part of good writing need not be limited to punctuation. Other kinds of accuracy, such as spelling, appropriate use of prepositions, and grammatical correctness, or features like mean length of sentence or successful collocation can also be treated in this way.

43   Supposing

FOCUS

This exercise helps students to become aware of a range of ways of introducing an additional hypothetical factor into a situation.

CLASS ORGANIZATION

Grouping: Students should sit in circles of six or seven. There should be one more person per group than the number of sentences that you are going to ask the students to write.
Time: 60 minutes.
Materials: None.

THE EXERCISE

1. Group the students and ask each student to think of an area where they feel their sophistication rating is low and where they wish they were more accomplished. Suitable areas include impressing members of the opposite sex, dress sense, at parties, handling the bank, complaining, in an expensive restaurant or travelling by air.

    Each student should briefly outline the area and the nature of their lack of sophistication on a sheet of paper – note-form is often best for this.

2. The sheet is then passed to the next member of the group, who writes a single sentence on it giving their colleague advice on how to become more sophisticated. The sentence must begin with the word 'Supposing...'

    The sheet continues to be passed round the circle, and at each movement an additional sentence is added on your instruction. Other suitable sentence starters include:

If ...	In order to ...
Were you to ...	Should ...
Unless ...	Imagine ...

    You may wish to take suggestions as to sentence starters from the class, and/or give instructions for sentences to be written to include rather than start with particular items (e.g., ...so that..., ... should...).

    For groups of seven, you need six sentence starters; for groups of six, you need five sentence starters, and so on.

3. Finally, the sheets end up with the students who first described their lack of sophistication – they can be read aloud, inaccuracies corrected and the advice commented on.

4. It is quite useful to have a homework follow-up. Two suggestions are:
    - Ask students to write a realistic paragraph under the title 'How to be better at...' using the sentence starters given and as many of the suggestions as are useful, together with their own supplementary material.
    - Ask students to write a paragraph under the title 'How to get on in my work' using the sentence starters practised in class.

COMMENTS

Students will be used to hearing tutors and supervisors start their sentences with, 'Supposing you were to...' and, 'If you were to...'. But how often do the students themselves in their own talking or writing modify an existing situation by first introducing a hypothetical factor? Can they find examples of this strategy in specialist academic texts? Why is this more common in spoken contexts than in written? In their examples, is the hypothesis or the existing situation more commonly found in the main or the subordinate clause, and is there a pattern in this?

Instruct students to think carefully about the appropriate linguistic form to choose to relate the kind of thought processes experienced in this exercise when they next experience them as writers.

44 Synthesis

FOCUS

Synthesis, or the ability to combine several simple sentences or thoughts into a more complex single sentence, is often a necessary skill in formal writing contexts. This is also an area of frustration for language learners whose intelligence may well enable them to see a logical relation between ideas which they cannot yet express in the target language. Those of us who have attained a moderate competence in a foreign language will recognize this demotivating phenomenon all too readily.

In the exercise that follows the learners provide topics to write about which are of real interest or concern to themselves; they are free to link together as many ideas as it seems possible or appropriate to link together and an opportunity is provided for fellow students to try to understand exactly what it is that the writer wants to say. Since there is no one 'right' synthesis of a set of simple sentences, the opportunity for rewriting and for experimentation that this exercise provides plays a crucial part in the process of learning to write.

CLASS ORGANIZATION

Grouping: Each member of the class will need to fill in a worksheet and complete the writing phase individually. Subsequently, the class works in small groups.

Time: 75 minutes.

Materials: Changes chart (see p.159).

THE EXERCISE

1. Each student should complete a Changes chart.
   Here is an illustration of what a completed chart might look like:

WORKSHEET: SYNTHESIS

CHANGES

	A change that occurred in the past	A change I'd like to see	For the following reason(s)
To my home/house	We moved away from the country **A1**	I'd like a garage **B1**	so that the car wouldn't be exposed to the elements **C1**
In my country	Abolition of capital punishment **A2**	The police shouldn't carry fire-arms **B2**	they are supposed to protect people not shoot them **C2**
In my job/work	I settled down **A3**	I'd like less responsibility **B3**	because I have too little time to myself at present **C3**
In my family	I left home when I was eighteen **A4**	To have a family holiday **B4**	Other families seem to enjoy them **C4**
In my financial situation	We had children and suddenly felt poorer **A5**	I'd like to grow rich **B5**	It would solve most of my problems **C5**

157

2. Next, three boxes (from different vertical and horizontal columns) should be selected more or less at random, and the student should attempt to see a previously unobserved connection between the three. For example, A5, B3 and C1:
   - we have two children which has made us poorer. (A5)
   - therefore I can't afford a garage (C1)
   - and therefore I have to take on a more responsible job than I'm suited to. (B3)

   Really ambitious students may choose a fourth box and try to relate its contents to those of the other three.
3. Once the students can see a logical connection between the three or four boxes, they should try to write a single sentence which captures this connection. For example, 'Since we have two children which has made us poorer, I can't afford ... and, more seriously, I have to take on ... '
4. In groups of six, students share their sentences in turn with other members of the group, making suggestions on how the wording might be improved to represent more exactly the logical relationships felt by the writer.

   Don't worry if only one or two sentences are explored in this way – it is often possible for students to learn far more from considering fellow-students' sentences than from having their own discussed.

COMMENTS

We suggest three ways of reinforcing the point practised in the exercise:
1. Ask students to take representative examples of an academic text in their subject area and of their own writing. How do the sentence lengths compare? What proportion of simple to complex sentences does the academic text contain? What possibilities for synthesis do they see in their own writing?
2. Ask students to consider when they are at the planning stage of their next piece of writing how the ideas that exist in note form might be linked together.
3. Ask students to take a complex sentence from the academic text they are currently reading and see what separate components it is made up of. In what other ways might these components have been synthesized? This exercise can be repeated each day for a week.

WORKSHEET: SYNTHESIS

CHANGES			
	A change that occurred in the past	A change I'd like to see	For the following reason(s)
To my home/ house	A1	B1	C1
In my country	A2	B2	C2
In my job/ work	A3	B3	C3
In my family	A4	B4	C4
In my financial situation	A5	B5	C5

Bibliography

Anathakrishnan, L. (1987) 'The Teaching of Writing in Malaysian Secondary Schools', unpublished M.A. dissertation, University of Durham.

Beach, R. & L. S. Bridwell (eds.) (1984) *New Directions in Composition Research*, Guilford Publications, U.S.A.

Bloor, T. & J. Norrish (eds.) (1987) *Written Language*, CILT for British Association of Applied Linguists.

Brookes, A. E. & P. Grundy (1988) *Designer Writing*, Pilgrims Publications, Canterbury.

Brookes, A. E. & P. Grundy (eds.) (1988) 'Individualization and Autonomy in Language Learning', ELT Documents 131, Modern English Publications, 1988.

Chenoweth, N.A. (1987) 'The need to teach rewriting', ELT Journal 41.1, 1987.

Clyne, M. (1987) 'Discourse structures and discourse expectations', in Smith, L. E. (ed.).

Coulthard, M. (ed.) (1986) *Talking about Text*, English Language Research, University of Birmingham.

Criper, A. and A. Davies (1986) 'Edinburgh ELTS Validation Project: Final Report', British Council, London, 1986.

Croft, K. (ed.) (1980) *Readings on English as a Second Language*, Winthrop (Cambridge, Mass.), Prentice Hall.

Dudley-Evans, T. (1986) 'Genre analysis: an investigation of the introduction and discussion sections of M.Sc. dissertations', in Coulthard, M. (ed.), 1986.

Dudley-Evans, T. (1988) 'One-to-one supervision of students writing MSc or PhD theses', in A. E. Brookes & P. Grundy (eds.), 1988.

Frederiksen, C. H. & J. F. Dominic (eds.) (1982) *Writing: The Nature, Development and Teaching of Written Communication (Vol. 2)*, Lawrence Erlbaum.

Freedman, A. (ed.) (1983) *Learning to Write: First Language/Second Language*, Longman.

Goodman, K. S. (1985) 'Transactional–psycholinguistic model: Unity in reading', in H. Singer and R. B. Ruddell (eds.), 1985.

Hamp-Lyons, L. and B. Heasley (1987) *Study Writing*, Cambridge University Press.

Hart's Rules for Compositors and Readers (1983) Oxford University Press.

Kachru, B. B. (ed.) (1986) *The Alchemy of English*, Pergamon.

Kaplan, R. B. (1972) 'Cultural thought-patterns in inter-cultural education', in K. Croft (ed.), 1972.

Kaplan, R. B. (1983) 'Contrastive rhetorics: some implications for the writing process', in A. Freedman (ed.), 1983.

Lloyd-Jones, R. (1981) 'Rhetorical choices in writing', in C. H. Frederiksen & J. F. Dominic (eds.), 1981.

Protherough, R. (1983) *Encouraging Writing*, Methuen.

Pugsley, J. (1988) 'Autonomy and individualisation in language learning: Institutional implications', in A. E. Brookes & P. Grundy (eds.), 1988.

Purves, A. (ed.) (1988) *Writing Across Languages and Cultures: Issues in Contrastive Rhetoric*, Sage Publications Ltd., London.

Raimes, A. (1983) 'Anguish as a second language? Remedies for composition teaching', in A. Freedman (ed.), 1983.

Regent, O. (1984) 'A comparative approach to the learning of specialized written discourse', in P. Riley (ed.), 1985.

Riley, P. (ed.) (1985) *Discourse and Learning*, Longman.

Shaughnessy, M. P. (1980) *Errors and Expectations*, Oxford University Press.

Singer, H. and R. B. Ruddell (eds.) (1985) *Theoretical Models and Processes of Reading*, International Reading Association.

St. John, M. J. (1987) 'Writing processes of Spanish scientists publishing in English', English for Special Purposes 6.2, 1987.

Stubbs, M. (1987) 'An educational theory of (written) language', in T. Bloor and J. Norrish (eds.), 1987.

Smith, L. E. (ed.) (1987) *Discourse across Cultures: Strategies in World Englishes*, Prentice Hall.

Swales, J. (1981) *Aspects of Article Introductions*, Aston Research Reports, University of Aston.

Further reading

In addition to these references we make two suggestions for further reading. The first is a teacher's resource book which contains many useful classroom ideas as well as a persuasive account of the writing process. The second is a series of course books containing several imaginative ideas.

Hedge, T. (1988) *Writing*, Oxford University Press.

Pincas, A. (1985) *Writing in English*, Macmillan.